TRANSITIONS
OF
THE
SOUL

Also by Nick Bunick

In God's Truth

About Nick Bunick

The Messengers
by Julia Ingram and G.W. Hardin

TRANSITIONS
OF
THE
SOUL

TRUE
STORIES
FROM
ORDINARY
PEOPLE

NICK BUNICK

HAMPTON ROADS
PUBLISHING COMPANY, INC.

Cover design by Steve Amarillo
Cover art, *Dispeller of Darkness,* by Ann Rothan

For information write:
Hampton Roads Publishing Company, Inc.
1125 Stoney Ridge Road
Charlottesville, VA 22902
Or call: 804-296-2772
Fax: 804-296-5096
e-mail: hrpc@hrpub.com
www.hrpub.com

If you are unable to order this book from your local bookseller, you may
order directly from the publisher.
Call 1-800-766-8009, toll-free.

Library of Congress Catalog Card Number: 00-108975
ISBN 1-57174-252-2
10 9 8 7 6 5 4 3 2

Printed on acid-free paper in Canada

Contents

Foreword

Like many of you, I have struggled often in my life with the challenge of understanding the purpose of life and death. I cannot tell you what day, what month, or what year the answers finally came to me, for it was a process that occurred over a long period of my life.

As I have traveled around the country and other parts of the world, I have become aware of a spiritual consciousness that is spreading like never before in the history of mankind. I have come to understand that our minds are the gateways to our hearts and souls. In addition, more and more people have opened their own gateways and are allowing information to come into their hearts and souls that ten years, five years, or even two years ago, they would not have allowed in.

I do not want to share with you my thoughts in metaphysical terms, but rather in terms that every one of us is capable of experiencing and understanding. At one time, there was a tremendous gap between New Age and mainstream thinking, but now that gap has become very small, and in many cases, you cannot distinguish between the two.

Perhaps the most important discovery I have made is that there is no such thing as death. Death is only a transition of our spirits and souls from the confinement of our physical bodies into the spiritual world. This new understanding is that we are not human beings which by coincidence have a spirit and soul, but we are spirits with a soul who are currently having a human experience.

Transitions of the Soul is meant to be shared with people from all walks of life, young and old, religious and nonreligious, mainstream and New Age, people from all ethnic backgrounds, regardless of social or economic positions. My hope is that once you have read *Transitions of the Soul,* you will see that death has indeed died.

The death I speak of is the concept found in the current Western world. We know that we and our loved ones will leave this mortal Earth plane someday; but what if we understood and embraced the answer to the universal question: Are we immortal and eternal? We would then know that our loved ones are still with us after their spirits have left their bodies. We would know that our loved ones want us to celebrate their lives through our memories of them, rather than mourn the passing over of their spirits. We would understand that they have been with us before and we shall someday be together again in the future. We would embrace the idea that as we approach our death, there is nothing to fear, for it is merely a doorway into the spiritual world where we will again be at one with God and in the company of our loved ones who have passed before us. We would know in our hearts that someday we will also be reunited with the loved ones we temporarily leave behind in this mortal world when we walk through that doorway ourselves.

The stories that you will find in *Transitions of the Soul* come from people of many walks of life. At times, you will shed tears of anguish and sadness, to be followed by tears of joy. You will experience the heartache as well as the love and the spiritual wisdom of the writers. But most important, you will have a totally different concept of death. On the day you realize this, indeed, the traditional concept of death will die.

Throughout the book, various writers occasionally mention the experiences they have with the number 444. If you have not read either of my previous books, *The Messengers* or *In God's Truth,* I would like to share with you that beginning in 1995, God intervened in my life using the numbers 444, which I now know is the symbol of the power of God's love. Since then, many thousands of our readers also have had 444 experiences. Although I will not discuss the 444 phenomenon with you at this time, I mention it only so you will have a little bit of understanding when some contributing writers mention a 444 experience.

God bless you all as you continue on your journeys.

Nick Bunick

Part One

Visitations

When I was a youngster, one of my friends who lived down the street shared an extraordinary story with me. Tony told me that his grandparents had been visiting their home, which was on the top floor of a three-story, three-family house. During that visit, his grandfather passed away.

My friend had no knowledge of the spiritual world. He was a ten-year-old street kid whose parent had come from Italy as young adults, and they barely spoke English. Tony told me he had a very loving and wonderful relationship with his grandfather, and three days after he had passed away, he appeared to Tony one night next to his bed. His grandfather told him not to grieve any further over his death. He said he was fine and that he would always be with him, looking after him and helping him. He said his grandfather was wearing the suit of clothes that he always wore when he was dressed up.

This was my first experience of having somebody share with me that they had a visitation from a loved one who had passed on.

I repeated this story to my mother, who was the youngest of seven children. My mother had psychic abilities, even though she did not know what the word meant, nor would she even acknowledge that she had this gift. She did tell me that she had been closer to her father than the other six older children, and had felt tremendous grief at his passing when she was merely a young adult. She told me that several days after his death, she woke up in the middle of the night and her father was sitting in a chair next to her bed. He reassured her that he was now in the spirit world, that he was doing fine, and there was no need for her to continue to feel pain over his passing on. My mother was absolutely positive that she had not been dreaming, and she shared with me in sincerity that her father had visited her after his death.

The following are a series of stories that have been provided to us by individuals who have had the spirit of a loved one visit them after their passing on. Some of these stories will make you cry with joy and others will make you laugh over their humor. But in all of the stories you will indeed recognize that what the writers experienced was not a fantasy, or a dream, but an actual visit from a loved one. You will know that for all these individuals, death has died.

Nick Bunick

You truly know that the spirit of God resides within you. You know with all of your heart and soul that you are a child of God. —In God's Truth

Chase

Blond, blue-eyed Chase came into the world two months too early. For this he suffered for the rest of his short life. With constant seizures and too much medication, he became limp as a rag doll, completely unable to move any part of his body. Sometimes he would smile at me, the corners of his mouth quivering with the strain of unused facial muscles.

When he became too big and sickly to care for, I placed him in a nursing home. It was the hardest thing I have ever done. Many years went by, and many late-night emergency phone calls, ambulance rides, and hospital stays. The nursing home wanted to have a feeding tube installed in Chase without the use of an anesthetic due to his condition. I flatly refused, and hired an attorney to make sure that Chase's painful life would never be artificially prolonged.

A year later, Chase began to die. He fought for each breath for four days. I had anticipated he would pass on in his sleep someday, and now I feared I had caused him even more pain. I was numb, but in the outside world around me it was spring and beautiful.

The night Chase died, he was thirteen years old, and the June full moon illuminated the sky. I sat next to the window in my dark living room, watching the moon and stars. "Where is he? Are you all right, Chase?" I had always been there for him in the past. Now he was alone, and he had been so out of it. How was he handling the transition? For the sake of his younger siblings, who were constantly tiptoeing into the room to hug me, I decided I should go to bed.

It was four A.M. when I got up to lock the front door. Looking out the window in the door, I noticed the crosses on top of each of the two neighboring churches. Both crosses were brilliantly ablaze. I had never seen that before. The next day, I checked them out, but both were just wooden crosses with no lights on them. For many years after that, I would check on the crosses, but they were never again lit up. Could it have been an answer from God to my question of whether Chase was okay?

A year later, caught up in the busy world of my three younger children, I seldom dwelled on Chase. The worst grieving had actually been when he was alive and suffering. I did, however, miss the joy I used to feel being with him.

Very late one night, I discovered I was sitting straight up in bed, but I did not remember waking or sitting up. I was just suddenly in that position. Instantly, I sensed I was not alone in the room. My mind said to run, for I was in fear. I began to toss the covers back so I could jump from the bed. Then I saw him standing at the foot of my bed. He was not the invalid thirteen-year-old, but a strong twenty-two-year-old, handsome and physically fit, smiling at his mother. His voice, which I had never heard before, calmly formed in my head. He simply said, "It's me."

Chase said, "I just came back to tell you I love you, and to thank you." Excitedly, I moved to wake the rest of the family. "No," was his response. "This is just for you." I told him I loved him, and I perceived he wanted me to go back to sleep. I laid my head back down and was instantly asleep.

The next morning, I thought, "What a great dream. It seemed so real." Everyone went off to school, and I began washing the morning dishes. Suddenly, I knew I was not alone in the room. Startled, I spun around. Chase was standing in the dining room. Now my eyes saw an energy mass about five feet tall. My mind, however, saw what he looked like, the young man of the night before. He telepathically said, "I just want to stay around the family for a few days." Answering out loud, I talked back to Chase as if he dropped in every day like this. It seemed perfectly natural, as if he had never died. He hung around and watched us for the next two days, but I did not tell the other kids, as I did not want to frighten them.

The morning of the third day arrived. I was sitting on the living room carpet with a take-home classroom test spread out on the coffee table before me, I was trying to concentrate. It was important for me to finish the test before my little boy bounced in the door from kindergarten. Chase was standing about eight feet to my left. In my head, I heard him say, "Look up." In a typical motherly fashion, answering him out loud, I said, "Just a minute."

"Look up," he repeated. I looked straight ahead at the clock, and knew I was running out of time to get my test done.

"Just a minute," I said again. In a more stern voice, he said for the third time, more slowly, "Look up now!" I turned my head and looked at him. He gently said, "They're coming for me now, and I won't be back." We exchanged "I love you" just as two balls of energy flew into the room, and just as quickly he flew out with them. I sat on the floor, stunned. The room seemed incredibly empty. That was six years ago, and Chase has never been back, at least where I can see and hear him.

He gave me a great gift those three days. I have never since grieved over him, but instead think of him as a young man capable of taking care of himself. Every once in a while, some wonderful little miracle will happen to us in conjunction with something to do with Chase, but that is another story. This story is how it came about that death no longer exists in my home.

Marilyn Lindell

Mother's Light

My mother died in 1996 at the age of seventy-two when an enlarged aorta burst. She had been living in a nursing home of her choice in Virginia. She had previously worked there as a practical nurse, so she knew the owners and staff well.

She was not ill when she arrived there, but she was unable to work any more and needed a good home. She had declared for years that she never wanted to live with any of us children, and we all had young families of our own. We thought this was a good decision, because she was very difficult to live with. Frankly, none of us would have been able to have her living in our home. Visiting for a week or weekend was a challenge, and that was the limit for us.

She had a private room and lived in the nursing home like one of the family, with full home privileges, coming and going as she pleased. Often she took a bus into Washington, D.C., for the day or weekend. The nursing home was nestled at the foothills of the Blue Ridge Mountains, and my mother loved the area, the beauty of the mountains, and of the home as well.

The enlarging aorta had been discovered a few years earlier. The doctor had told her she had five to ten years to live. He told her the bursting would happen so fast, she would be gone in a second. He told her that during the years leading up to her death, there would be no pain or illness.

One day, she pulled down the window shades in her room, blocking out all of the sunlight. She refused to eat or leave her room, and stopped reading her beloved mystery stories. That night, she lay in her bed in a darkened room. If someone turned on the lights, she would put them out the moment they left the room. Her mail sat on the dresser unopened. So it went for the last year of her life. The doctor said there was nothing he could do about it, because she had decided to die, even though there was no physical reason for this behavior.

I went to visit her one evening in the fall. The owner of the nursing home had kept in close communication with me, so I knew what to expect. I went into the room with my usual cheeriness, asking why in the world she was lying there in the dark. Although I had had a full description of her appearance, I was stunned to see her near-skeletal condition. She looked so tiny, and her face was sunken almost beyond recognition. I could not believe that in the few short weeks since I had last visited, she had deteriorated to such an extent. I was able to keep my voice cheery and natural, but I dreaded sharing the news I was bearing, that my husband and I and our family had to move to Houston. As I had feared, she hated the news; but she took it quite well. We talked for some time. When I left, I knew I would never see her again.

She died in January. I was told that she yelled for the nurse, who was just leaving her room, but that she had passed over by the time the nurse returned to her bedside. Indeed, the bursting aorta took her in a moment. Even so, she had lived fifteen years past the doctor's prediction.

Although we had learned long ago of her approaching death, we still had quite a measure of shock and plenty of grief. This was hard for me to understand. Before I had attended school, I believed we had all lived before. I believed we would live again in another body, and that only the body died. I knew this in my heart, although not as a fact. By the time of my mother's death, I had been introduced to Edgar Cayce's work, and many such heartfelt beliefs were now truths, as far as I was concerned.

In any case, her passing was very sad for me. I kept thinking that she had had mostly a very lonely, unhappy life, especially after her divorce from my father many years earlier. On the other hand, I would remind myself that now she was free. She was in the spiritual world, reunited with her sisters and family who had already crossed over. Then the grief would overcome me again. Back and forth I went, from happiness for her release to terrible grief. Making my feelings worse was the fact that I am empathic. I have the gift of being able to tune in to other people, to feel other people's feelings. Most often, I am not confident about the thoughts I receive, but I am certain as to how others feel. But I could not bring myself to tune in to Mom.

Three days after her death, in the middle of the night, I was lying on my back with my left hand resting on my stomach. I was gently awakened by the warm touch of a hand on my left hand. I thought it was probably one of my children needing something, although they usually tapped me softly until my eyes opened. I looked up and was astonished, for my mother was standing over me! She looked very young, maybe in her forties, and very, very beautiful, smiling happily like I had never seen before.

She was wearing a lovely colorful flower-print dress, and her hair was light brown, curled perfectly. There were no actual words spoken, but clearly she was telling me how very happy she was, and that she was glad to be right where she was, like it was all wonderful and I should not have another sad thought about her passing.

The longer I watched her, the more excited I became, until suddenly I could not see her anymore, but I still felt the warmth of her hand. Then she was gone. I was elated. I wanted to dance around the bedroom in joy, around the whole house. To be sure, there was no more sleeping for me that night.

My grief was gone, and never did I have it again. It was such an astonishing experience, one I have always cherished. However, in the back of my mind, I knew there was something unusual about the way my mother had looked. But I could not, for the life of me, put my finger on what it was.

At least six months later, it hit me out of the blue.

Mother had visited me in the middle of the night, and the only light in the bedroom was a bit of light flowing through the door, which was barely opened. I kept it that way in case one of the children needed me, so they could see their way into my room. But my mother had been in her own light. She had been surrounded by light in a very dark room. It was not a spotlight, though; it was her own light!

That is the end of the incredible experience of seeing my mother the first time after her passing. I have seen her since in my dreams, but that is another story. I would like to add that there is no way in this beautiful world I would have ever shared this story with anyone other than Nick Bunick. I have many friends I have never shared such "far-out" experiences with; but for Nick, who had the courage to tell his huge, beautiful story, I can share mine. Also, I know the angels can validate the truthfulness of it. How great is that?

Barbara Furniss Bauer

In reality, the spirit world is a continuous revolving door into the physical world. Or, if you prefer, the physical world is a continuous revolving door into the spiritual world.
                                                    —In God's Truth

I Am Never Alone

The spring of 1992 found my husband Vince and me shopping for a home for the first time in our twenty-three years of marriage. It seemed like a fun way to spend the afternoon. Our family of four sons had grown and were living on their own, so now it was our turn.

The California day was perfect, and the homes we saw were all beautiful, but not quite right. That is, until we walked into the one that obviously had been built with us in mind. It was love at first sight. It would be a sweet home to retire in. We pooled all our resources, sold a car, had a couple of yard sales, and moved into our beautiful new home on July 17, 1992.

Eight months later, while we were still decorating our new home, Vince was diagnosed with oral cancer and given only six months to live. I'd heard that pronouncement before, sitting in a theater eating popcorn, but the people on the movie screen were paid to say that to each other. This was not something I expected to hear in real life. There had to be another line in the script.

My heart screamed, "Somebody say something!" The doctor's mouth moved, but the words "six months to live" had deafened both of us. Occasionally, words came through, such as "surgery," "put your things in order," "take a cruise."

First the vise grips your head, your throat goes dry instantly, your heart beats so loudly that you're sure everyone in the room can hear it and knows the sentence you've been given. Then the numbness sets in. Now I know all too well what people mean when they talk about a knot in the pit of their stomach. That description fits like no other. You go through the motions of living. Sleep would be a kind blessing, but you can't even do that.

After three or four days of just holding hands, we began to talk, each of us afraid of the next word. Death had never been discussed before in front of my husband. It was not a subject he would tolerate, and even at that point, we were still dancing around it.

While the doctors cleared their schedules for testing, surgery, et cetera, we went to the movies, to any comedy we could find, sometimes one or two a day. It was a great year for comedies, so we were fortunate to manage a few smiles.

Realization finally set in. We were emerging from our numbing cocoons, and began to talk and plan. We informed our family, and started to plan for the inevitable, and we prayed. Having done and said all we could, we set out to make each day count.

Over the next two and a half years, Vince underwent sixteen surgeries and displayed courage and compassion like I had never seen before, even though I always had known in my heart it was there. He made doctors and nurses laugh and never took his ailment seriously. He felt bad for those who were uncomfortable with his progressive disfigurement, so he made fun of himself in order to ease others' discomfort. He didn't complain about his increasing pain, or give in to the "why me?" question. His reasoning through the whole ordeal was that "Jesus suffered more."

In that two and a half years of growing together, we shared a lifetime of experiences. Colors became brighter, laughter sounded more joyful, and family was more than precious. It was strange how we all suddenly were able to clear our busy schedules to spend more time together and enjoy what was truly important. Under normal circumstances, we would have denied ourselves this simple pleasure. Everything had meaning, including our conversations about death. We spoke of death by reexamining our lives. We focused on how we had lived and whom we had touched. Death was no longer feared like a fire-breathing dragon, but became the door through which we pass into eternal life. We saw that death is the progression of life, that in dying we are born to eternal life.

Vince passed away on October 30, 1995. His sons, their families, and I stood around the hospital bed giving him loving support, and we were all touching some part of him as he stepped across that threshold. The nurses, in trying to help during those last few moments, were unintentionally causing him more discomfort. Being the trooper that he was, he kept trying to hang on for their sakes. I interrupted the confusion by loudly saying, "Honey, I love you. The family is all here and we'll be okay if you want to go now."

One of the nurses gasped. He gave us a familiar thumbs-up as we chanted, "We're okay, go, Dad, go." He lay back and the heart monitor became quiet. I felt his release as though it were my own. No more pain! Vince embraced death with his thumbs-up gesture, indicating his readiness to go on.

At his funeral, a friend of my son's came to me to offer his condolences. "I never met your husband, but your son has told me many stories of what a wonderful man he was. I'm sorry for your loss," he said. I found myself smiling and responded, "Oh, if you never met him, I'm sorry for your loss."

The gathering afterward was at our home. The younger children were playing in the front yard while music and laughter could be heard from within. The stories exchanged all began with, "Remember when." The postman was doing his rounds when he remarked to my son outside, "I knew your dad was pretty sick, but from the party, it looks like he's doing better, huh?" My son said, "Yes, he is."

Four years have gone by, and I can still feel Vince's presence whenever I choose. My ten-year-old grandson Brian quietly told me the other day, "Grandpa came to visit me the other night. I was in bed and I wasn't feeling very good. He patted me on the head like Grandpa did and rubbed my back with his big hand until I felt better."

With a warm glow in my heart, I encouraged him. "Grandpa tells me he visits you often, Brian." His eyes lit up. I started to walk away and he called after me, "Grandma, tell him I said thanks, okay?" I smiled and said, "Sure I will." Brian responded with a thumbs-up and said, "Cool."

I am awakening to a greater love and power within. My husband's gift to me was my freedom. I read spiritual books, attend classes and lectures, and interact with those who understand that a purposeful life enriches each one of us. I am hungry for the love of God and the joys of life, and willingly share all bits of wisdom that pass through me.

Vince, I am proud to be your widow. I know we all passed this one with angelic colors. I am one, but I am never alone.

Claire Gardner

The Rock of Gibraltar

My father was the kind of man who was passionate about life. Not just his life, but others' as well. This sometimes irritated more than a few people.

Ted was my father's name, and he was very robust and animated, smiling all the time. He seemed to have answers for everything. Our family viewed him as a genius. Though not a holy man, he attended church at the Roman Catholic cathedral, mesmerizing all who were lucky enough to attend, hearing the magic of his voice as he sang "The Lord's Prayer" and "Bless This House."

My mother and we six kids always dreaded the fateful day when our dad would die, knowing that Heaven would gain a most beautiful angel and the Earth would be an emptier place without him. My dad's heart was never very good. He had already outlived everyone in his Albanian family, so we knew that with his passion for food, it was only a matter of time before his body gave out.

In 1997, the fears that had plagued me all my life came to a blinding reality when Dad suffered his second heart attack at age seventy-seven. I was pregnant at the time. Dad went into the hospital for open-heart surgery to unclog the arteries that were killing him. He suffered a stroke on the operating table. I will never get the picture out of my mind of him lying there so helpless. Our family's "Rock of Gibraltar" was slipping away, and in such a humiliating way. The left side of Dad's face and throat was paralyzed, so he could no longer do the things that he enjoyed the most: talk, sing, laugh, and eat.

On the night of July 16, 1997, my twin sister Kim, my older sister Sue, my mother, and I had an overwhelming feeling to go see Dad—to tell him to fight if he wanted to come home and that there is nothing impossible if your will wants it badly enough. Dad died that night, and so, it seemed, did my reason for living. I cannot begin to describe the emptiness and sadness that were with me every hour of every day. I could not get rid of the picture of my father, once so robust and full of life, lying in the hospital with tubes up his nose, thin as a rail, and so frail-looking. It killed me to see him like that.

For many months, I would cry, wishing I had told him how proud I was of him for going through that torture. Then one night, my father came to see me. It sounds unbelievable, I know, but as I lay awake in my bed staring up at the ceiling, his face filled the room over my bed and he said, "Why do you cry and cry?" I blurted out all the things that were making me sad about him dying, and I told him how much I missed him. Then he said the most amazing thing to me. He told me that he had heard my brother David complaining that his girlfriend had hurt his feelings yesterday (which was true) and how David was cursing his life and the world.

Dad then said to me with all the passion that he could muster, "Do you not realize how blessed you are to feel 'hurt' while you are on Earth? I will tell you how blessed you are. Where I am there is peace, but I tell you this: I am not able to taste melted butter on a hot piece of French toast, feel warm watermelon running down my chin, or smell the wood fire on a crisp October day. I will never feel a spring breeze on my face. I can't touch the engine of a car or feel the grease between my fingers or touch the wing of a plane before I fly it. Do you understand?"

His voice boomed. "Don't you realize that every feeling, good or bad, is a blessing that you can only experience while in your physical body? Yes, I hear your questions when you ask, 'Dad, why do you sound so unemotional? Can't you remember what it was like to lose a loved one? Why does everyone from the Other Side always say, 'Stop crying,' when it seems like none of you can remember how it is to deal with death and pain?'

"Emotion is a physical blessing that you have and I don't," said Dad. "I see you and hear you and love you, and please know that I am safe, happy, and peaceful. Though I looked frail and humiliated in the hospital to you, that was not how I felt. I was preparing to go home, and my body was simply shutting down. When you used to ride that horse of yours and you'd run across the field and get off, your sisters would say, 'Whew, Tammy, you looked like you were riding a fire-breathing dragon! Are you all right?' And you would look at them with a puzzled face, because it looked scary even though it wasn't at all. Wasn't it exhilarating? You bet it was! It was the most exciting time of your life, right? You would not trade the experience of doing it for anything, right?

"It is the same thing when the body closes down. Some of you don't understand what a small detail it is in the whole picture of the journey of our souls. It makes you hold on to the picture that you remembered, trying to imagine what 'closing down' is like. It's wonderful! I can't tell you how blessed I am to have been able to experience that."

My father always could talk a lot, but I am glad that this time I listened to the message he gave me, so that I may share it with many others. His message is of truth, love, and the power of God, about being thankful every day for pleasures and pains. The day I got his message was the blessed day that death died for me.

Tammy McGowan

I'll Be There in Spirit

Our family has gained great reassurance and comfort from my mother's experiences associated with the passing of her father in 1961. My mother, who shortly will celebrate her ninetieth birthday, has been sustained over the years by her spiritual closeness with her father.

My wife Ronelle and I visited my grandfather in the hospital late in 1961, about five weeks before our wedding day, January 5, 1962. To cheer him, we said we were looking forward to having him well so he could attend our wedding. Smiling, he said, "I will not be able to attend your wedding, but I will be there in spirit." That was the last time we saw him, as he passed over a few days later, less than one month before we were married.

Some years later, we were talking with my mother about my grandfather, Charles, and we mentioned what he had said about being there "in spirit." Mom became quite excited as she told us of her experience during our marriage ceremony. Her father had been a clergyman for over sixty years until his death at eighty-five years of age. He always wore the gown and clerical collar when he took services. While she was sitting quietly as our wedding ceremony began, she suddenly became aware that her father was standing with his hand on the church altar. Mom said she was amazed, and started to say, "Oh, there's Dad," but at that moment, he vanished from her sight.

His spiritual appearance had given her the reassurance

she sought at the time regarding our marriage, while the knowledge of her experience gave us all encouragement about the continuity of life in both physical and spiritual form.

Marc Faulks

The Little Girl

There came a frantic knock at the doctor's office door,
A knock more urgent than he had ever heard before,

"Come in, come in," the impatient doctor said.
"Come in, come in, before you wake the dead."

In walked a frightened little girl, a child no more than nine.
It was plain for all to see, she had troubles on her mind.

"Oh doctor, I beg you, please come with me.
My mother is surely dying, she's as sick as she can be."

"I don't make house calls, bring your mother here."
"But she's too sick, so you must come or she will die, I fear."

The doctor, touched by her devotion, decided he would go.
She said he would be blessed, more than he could know.

She led him to her house, where her mother lay in bed,
Her mother was so very sick she couldn't raise her head.

But her eyes cried out for help, and help her the doctor did.
She would have died that very night had it not been for her kid.

The doctor got her fever down and she lived through the night.
Morning brought the doctor signs that she would be all right.

The doctor said he had to leave but would return again by two,
And later he came back to check, just like he said he'd do.

The mother praised the doctor for all the things he'd done.
He told her she would have died, were it not for her little one.

"How proud you must be of your wonderful little girl,
It was her pleading that made me come; she's really quite a pearl!"

"But doctor, my daughter died over three years ago,
Is the picture on the wall of the little girl you know?"

The doctor's legs went limp, for the picture on the wall
Was the same little girl for whom he'd made this call.

The doctor stood motionless for quite a little while,
And then his solemn face was broken by his smile.

He was thinking of that frantic knock heard at his office door,
And of the beautiful little angel that had walked across his floor.

This is a beautiful poem of love and light. The author chose to remain anonymous. —Ed.

My Daughter

The first Saturday evening in September 1995, I sat down to meditate. I was seven and a half months pregnant and deeply concerned because I had not felt my baby move for several days. As I placed my hands on my belly and settled in, a soft voice came to me and said, "She is dying."

This was too shocking and painful for me to accept, so I denied it fiercely. Three days later, I went in for a prenatal exam and learned that, yes, my baby had died! Words cannot adequately express the wailing grief of losing a baby.

My husband and I had our daughter's body cremated. We took her ashes and buried them at the base of an ancient tree, deep in the heart of the old growth near where we lived.

I was grieving deeply as I said my good-byes, and finally, exhausted, I leaned back against the tree. A peace and calm washed over me, and then my daughter's spirit came to me and said, "You and Fred [my husband] were not who I needed you to be for me to be who I needed to be. You can stop grieving now, for I will come back to you again as your child."

This was a powerful, transformational moment in my life. I was able to release my pain and move into wonder and hope. And I know for certain that no one ever dies.

Lisa Cahall Swisher

The Truth

As long as I can remember, I have known the truth. My parents spoke of it many times. Through my life, the truth was repeated over and over to me, ever strengthening my belief. It had a major impact on my life, and it is because of this that I believe I am still living today. It was the truth, and it led me into my journey of spirituality that I am still on today.

My story began one night in the late 1940s, when my parents and grandparents were sitting around the kitchen table, talking. The subject of death came up. One by one, they explained what they expected and what they would want to happen upon the event of death in their lives. The thought of life after death was discussed, and they all vowed to each other that whoever passed first would come back to show the others that there was life after death. About six months later, my grandmother passed away suddenly of heart failure.

Several unexplainable things happened surrounding her death. The night after the funeral, all of the family was shaken up, so they stayed at her home. The next morning, to their astonishment, in the middle of the living room stood a picture of my grandmother. The first one who saw this woke the rest, and they were all amazed. Each one thought that perhaps the others had put it there, but they all swore they had not.

The next experience was more incredible.

My mother got up early one morning to make coffee and breakfast for my father. As she walked downstairs and started for the kitchen, she looked up. There stood my grandmother in full-blown life. My mom shook her head and blinked her eyes, and my grandmother smiled at her. Mom quickly ran upstairs to tell my dad, but when she got there, he sat up in bed and said to her, "You just saw my mother." They were both in shock, for he had seen her too.

I was born in 1950, and years later, my dad came home from work one day and walked into my nursery to say hello, and there was my grandmother standing over me, smiling.

This and the other experiences were told over and over to me during my life. They have inspired my spirit and my journey, so that I know without a doubt that there truly is life after death.

In 1996, I was diagnosed with leukemia and knew I had a tremendous fight ahead of me. It is because of my spiritual beliefs that I am still here today to write about this. Yes, doctors and nurses played a big part, but I believe that my role as a believer played an enormous part in my recovery. My willpower and the magic of believing have helped me overcome the tremendous pain and depression. I knew that I had help from above. I knew that God was ever present with me and that my angels were by my side. Knowing and believing made it possible for me to endure going through two bone marrow transplants.

I know that death is not the end. It is only a transition of our spirit. Thank you for letting me tell my story.

Kathleen Ellstrom

Mom's Special Gifts

When I was growing up, my mom and grandmother talked about relatives who had died but who came back with messages all the time. It was never a frightening thought. I realized my mom had a gift. She was obviously very open to communication with spirits because she had great faith and was not afraid. Let me give you some examples:

Mom was the youngest of seven children. She was born when my grandmother was forty-five and my grandfather fifty-two. She was a true change-of-life baby. Her nearest sibling was thirteen years older, and her older brothers had children of their own when Mom was born. Mom's niece, Elizabeth, who was older than my mother, died while giving birth to her child. At the time, Mom and Dad were newly married and shared a duplex with my grandparents. Dad worked nights as a baker. One night after my mother had just gotten into bed, Elizabeth appeared to her. She asked Mom to please tell Lester, her husband, that she was not dead, that she was well and not to worry about her. She just wanted Lester to take care of the baby.

My parents moved to New Jersey when I was three years old. My grandparents moved with us, but my grandfather, Opa, died three months after the move. Just weeks after that, my mother came into my room to see if I was covered. She looked out into the hall, and Opa was standing there, holding the hand of my father's younger brother. Opa told my mother to tell Dad that he would take care of his brother.

This was startling because my dad's brother was still alive. Two hours later, my aunt called to say Dad's brother had died.

I am sure all this sounds rather frightening, but my family took these as true signs from Heaven.

I was a participant in one of Mom's happenings. It was a summer day and Mom was in the dining room. She told my grandmother that someone rode into the yard on a bicycle, and said laughingly, "It looks like our Ernst," a cousin from Germany. She said he wore a black turtleneck and black pants. Then Mom told me to go out and see who it was, but no one was out there. That afternoon, the mailman brought an envelope from Germany telling my grandmother that Ernst had died. He had been killed in an accident.

I find all this very comforting and reassuring. My parents talked all of the time about healers and people with visions. I believe that individuals who are open and unafraid receive messages that others are too closed or frightened to receive, and I believe that this gift is inherited, be it through DNA or whatever.

As for my own communications, I either hear them or write them. The words appear in language balloons, like in cartoons. When I asked who my guardian angel was, the word "Isaiah" appeared several days later. Many times, a voice awakens me. One morning, it shouted, "Watch out for it!" But it wasn't until a year later that the mirror above our bed fell off the wall in the middle of the night.

I have received signs about the upcoming birth of my own grandchildren, even before they were conceived. Only once did I "see" something. I had asked several times to visit my grandmother, who had passed on. A being who radiated bright blue light said he was there to take me to see her, but I was too afraid to go.

There is no doubt in my mind that our angels are watching over us constantly.

Myra Z. Johnson

They [the angels] also told me the numbers 444 would play a very important part of my life, as well as the lives of others. They said that 444 represented the power of God's love. —In God's Truth

Curtis

No one suspected he was an angel. He had lived a difficult childhood, followed by drug and alcohol abuse later in life. I did not know him then, so I had no preconceived notions about who Curtis was, or was not.

We met through our respective partners, who happened to be working at a psychic hotline. Gloria invited my partner Erik and me to a spiritual circle. It sounded like what we had been looking for. We had been searching for like-minded, spiritual people who were open to New Age ideas such as Erik and I often discussed at length. We had hoped to find a community of friends with whom we could share these ideas. We went with open minds and hearts. We felt at ease in this group, although we had never previously tried spirit mediumship. The spiritual circle brought me a sense of peace and belonging that I had never before experienced.

It was to be several months before we met again the following February, this time at Curtis and Gloria's new home. Over the next few months, we met weekly for the spiritual circle at Just-2-Be, the name they had given to the circle group and to their new mini-farm. That is exactly what it came to be for me, a place just to "be." It was a place where I felt I was more myself than at any other place I had ever been. At the circle each week, I would renew my faith in the divine, gather my thoughts and strength, and occasionally receive messages for other people in the group.

It did not come easily. Spirit connection takes work, dedication, and faith. During this time, Curtis always encouraged me, gave me ideas on how to maintain the spiritual connection, and gently pushed me into areas of healing or mediumship he thought would be beneficial for my growth. Often during our circle, I would sense Curtis helping and guiding me on a spiritual path, and offering guidance as my mind wandered and tried to connect with spirit. These were unspoken encounters. I never mentioned these experiences, and neither did he.

Oftentimes, one of the other members of the circle would remark that he could sense an angel above Curtis and me, especially if we happened to be sitting next to each other. Neither of us commented on this. I kept these experiences close to my heart, and my spiritual connection with Curtis grew stronger.

In July, Gloria asked us if we could pick up any messages about Curtis's health. He had been having trouble swallowing and keeping food in his stomach. He was to see a doctor the following week. It was at that appointment that Curtis learned he had a malignant tumor on his esophagus. It was his thirty-ninth birthday.

Over the next six months, Curtis went through radiation, chemotherapy, and surgery. I started giving him regular Reiki treatments. I gave him a treatment each week before the spiritual circle met and sometimes additional treatments during the week. Sometimes other Reiki practitioners would join me. I asked for guidance and help. I started opening up more, and my connection to spirit became stronger. I received many different messages about healing for Curtis. In one mediation, I received a detailed method of using crystals laid out in an intricate circular grid under some pine trees in his backyard. During that Reiki session, other people from the Spiritualist Church, where Curtis was a very active member, sent healing to him also. That spot still holds a very strong healing energy to this day, over a year later.

By this time, I had received my Reiki Master degree, and trained both Curtis and Gloria so he could have Reiki on a daily basis. During another healing session, I received messages and guidance from a blue angel called Ramel. I believe him to be the same angel that had been seen over us at the spiritual circle. It was during this session that I realized that Curtis was not going to stay with us in the physical world. Even though he said he wanted to fight the cancer, I felt that his soul was ready to pass over. This was overwhelming for me. I did not discuss it with anyone for some time, not even Curtis. I was hoping it was not true. Perhaps it was only a possible future outcome I had seen. I hoped that with diligent intent and healing effort, what I had seen could be erased from the future. But it was not to be.

Curtis was feeling stronger after Christmas and returned to work. He had been working less than a week when he started dropping things, and his step was unsteady. When he returned to the oncologist, new, fast-growing tumors were found on his brain and liver. We later learned that the doctor had given him no hope of survival. Curtis never told anyone the prognosis. The doctors recommended radiation for the brain tumor and then large doses of chemotherapy to possibly extend his life.

Even though he was aware of the alternatives available to him, Curtis felt very strongly that he was supposed to follow the healing route that the doctors suggested. The radiation helped with the brain tumor so he could think more clearly, and his motor skills returned to a more normal level. However, he was still weak and tired from the radiation when the chemotherapy began, and he became markedly worse. The side effects from the chemotherapy made him very ill, but he continued to try to maintain a normal schedule. He worked around the farm and at the church, and he continued to maintain a positive outlook whenever we met.

The end of July was camp week at the Spiritualist Church. Curtis and Gloria had arranged for me to speak about Reiki. Curtis rode with me to the church. He was quiet that day, and he seemed very weak. He talked about seeing images and doors to other worlds in the clouds. When I gave him Reiki after my presentation, I could not feel any energy from his waist down to his feet. All of his energy, a beautiful blue-white light, was around his heart and head. When I left him that day, he hugged me for a long time and said, "Good-bye. I love you, honey." He always called me "honey." It was a term of endearment, like I was a kid sister, even though I was two years his elder. But that day it felt different. The emphasis had been on "good-bye."

I looked him in the eye to see if he had meant what I suspected. He kissed my forehead and gently moved me toward the car. Tears were streaming down my face as I pulled away from the church. That was the last time I saw him in a coherent state. It was the day before his fortieth birthday.

The following week, I was very busy with Reiki classes and other commitments. I called and arranged to visit Curtis and Gloria on Thursday for a Reiki treatment. On Thursday morning, Gloria called to tell me she was taking Curtis to the hospital because he was dehydrated, and asked me to meet them at the hospital after work. She called back later in the afternoon to tell me the hospital had sent him home. There was nothing they could do for him. It would not be long before he passed over. I stopped at Just-2-Be after work and gave Curtis and Gloria some Reiki. I am not sure if Curtis knew I was there. He was in and out of consciousness. I silently told him it was okay to go.

Early Monday morning, Gloria called to tell me that Curtis had passed over the night before. I was surprised. It seemed so quick. No matter how long you anticipate that moment, knowing that it can come at any time, it always seems like a surprise when it actually happens. Somewhere in the back of your mind you are still hoping that something will change, that a miracle will happen and your loved one will not leave you.

That morning after learning of Curtis's death, I went to a place where I often meditate. It is a beautiful spot and has always been special to me. There is a small lake and beyond that a mountain. That day, the lake was serene, as smooth as glass. I climbed onto my favorite rock, meditated, and cried. Many mournful sounds erupted from my soul and echoed across the lake and mountains. The Earth heard me and understood. She took my pain and held me close to her bosom. Three ravens joined me for a while in a call and response of love and loss for a dear friend. It was a magical experience on many levels. I felt Curtis's energy near me. By then, after the many Reiki sessions, I was familiar with his energy and how it reacted with my own. He was clearly near me. I could feel him, without a doubt. Perhaps this was just my way of coping with his death, to deny that he was actually gone.

After a couple of hours, I felt I was ready to visit Gloria. I had needed this time alone to release my sorrow and gather my strength to help her. The distance between my home and Just-2-Be is about forty-five miles, of which forty miles is desolate highway. There are three village oases along the way, and my car happened to break down at one of them that day. This in itself was a miracle to me. I could have broken down anywhere on that deserted road. Why there?

I managed to get the car to a garage and they agreed to fix it right away. The woman who ran the office was an open and warm person, and we struck up a conversation immediately. Around noon, she went next door to the store to get a sandwich and asked if I would like anything. I told her I would wait until my car was off the lift because my purse was in the car. She said, "Don't be crazy," and handed me a five dollar bill. She said, "Here, take this and buy what you want. You can pay me back when your purse gets freed." I thanked her, took the money, and went to the store.

When I walked into the store, I felt as if I had landed in an oasis. The couple who ran the store chatted warmly with me while they made me a sandwich. I got a drink from the cooler and brought it to the cash register. When the woman rang up my lunch, the total came to $4.44. I was so shocked, I stood there for a few seconds without moving. Finally, I said to her, "Do you know that is an angel number?" Immediately, I heard Curtis's voice saying, "You are the angel, honey."

It was so clear that I spun around to look behind me. I turned and looked at the woman at the cash register to see if she had heard it. She was standing there with my change, looking at me a bit askance. I looked behind me again, just to be sure. There was no one else in the store, but I was certain I had heard it. There was no question in my mind that it was Curtis's voice. Once again, I could feel his energy, as if he were standing next to me. It was so real, yet so unbelievable. I took my change and stumbled out of the store, trying to make sense of what I had just experienced. He really was not "dead," and he was trying to prove it to me in a way I would believe. After that experience, I believed!

Since then, I have felt Curtis near me often and have received clear messages from him. I have also received messages from my other guides regarding Curtis and the meaning of his life and our relationship. Our Reiki sessions allowed us time to be still and to connect with each other on a spiritual level so that I would be able to recognize him when he had passed over. He felt that he could do much better spiritual work from where he is now than from here on the Earth. Existence is difficult here, and sometimes even the best-laid plans for growth do not work out in the physical realm the way we imagine them when we are in spirit. Curtis plans to work with me through Reiki and other modes of healing in the future. Together we can be a powerful healing team for helping others. I have already begun to feel him near me during Reiki sessions. He offers guidance about hand placements and helps me by joining with my energy for a higher vibration and deeper healing for the client on both a physical and spiritual level.

I knew Curtis only a short time, less than two years, yet I feel I have known him forever. He came into my life when I most needed spiritual guidance and growth. He taught me to believe in and to open up to the spiritual realms that he navigated with such ease. Because we established this spiritual connection, the transition was easier for me to accept. I know that he truly is not gone. He is just in a different form. He continues to be my guide and teacher as long as I remember to listen with an open heart.

One of the things that we pray for in the spiritual circle is spiritual progression or growth for those who have passed over. A short time after Curtis died, I asked for his progression during a meditation. My guides smiled and told me he did not need too much progression, since he already had his "wings" long before he passed over. Truly, as Erik once told me, guardian angels come in all forms. I have had the special blessing of knowing mine first here in the physical, and now in the spiritual.

Sandra Linton

The Funeral

For many years, I have believed that death is not a turning out of the lights, an end to life, but rather a beginning, the rebirth into another level of consciousness. However, belief did not turn to knowing until I had an incredible experience regarding my first husband at his funeral in 1972. What happened was a turning point of knowing for me. I haven't shared this story with many people, mostly because I don't enjoy seeing an expression of disbelief followed by the "this-lady-is-a-nut" look. If someone else can be helped, then being considered strange is a small price to pay. But first, a little background may be needed.

My husband Vic and I were divorced in the mid-1960s after twenty-six years of marriage. In those days, people didn't break up their marriages just because they were unhappy. We had sweated it out because we accepted our responsibility to our children (we had two sons). We felt that they shouldn't suffer for our mistakes, so we gave our boys our best effort. However, when they were grown, out of school, and married, it was our turn. Vic and I had grown apart and had entirely different interests, except for our children, and it seemed we didn't even speak the same language. We no longer understood each other. I felt he was more concerned about his personal needs than about the family. He claimed, rightly, that I nagged and expected too much from him. The marriage failed in spite of some effort at receiving counseling.

I remarried in 1969 and was very happy. Vic was engaged to a fine woman, and I was pleased for him. There was no acrimony, and it seemed we could get along well enough to be friends and grandparents without being married any longer. We never got that far, because he died unexpectedly of a massive heart attack in the summer of 1972.

Our sons and their wives arrived from out of town to stay with my new husband and me while they made arrangements to lay their father to rest. At the funeral service, I sat by myself at the back of the family room; our sons and their wives sat on seats in front of me. A sheer curtain hung at the front of this area, separating it from the chapel, where we could see Vic in his casket and the minister waiting by the podium to start the services. Off to one side, a vocalist was singing a hymn.

My thoughts were centered on my children, and I noted that grief was evident in their body language and faces. It had been a long time since I had seen tears in their eyes, and my heart went out to them. If I could only comfort them and make it well, like I did when they were little. At the podium, the minister began to speak, and his words broke through my reverie as he talked of the meeting that could be expected on the day the dead rise from their graves. I wondered what my sons' thoughts were on this subject and wished I'd been a little more pointed in telling them what I believed, which basically was that the death Vic had endured was not a permanent thing.

Whether there was a physical movement or just the shift in my consciousness to another level, I'm not sure, but all of a sudden I became aware that Vic was sitting to my immediate right. That he was there didn't surprise me. It seemed so natural. His left arm was extended behind me on the railing of the chair. He sat in the same relaxed fashion that I had seen many times before, his right leg bent at the knee and his foot and ankle resting on his left knee. What jarred my sensibilities far more than seeing him was the fact that he was laughing almost uncontrollably. He seemed to realize that I was tuned in to his presence, and as he turned to look at me, his laughter dropped to a chuckle.

My thoughts formed words, and intuitively I knew we could communicate that way. With as frosty a tone as I could muster, considering I couldn't speak, I asked, "And what is so funny?"

Vic motioned with his right arm toward the front of the family room, to our sons grieving just a few feet from where we sat, to the minister speaking beyond the sheer curtain, and to his physical body resting in the casket. "It's just so damn funny," he said, and dissolved in laughter again. His relief at being conscious, knowing and feeling at his own funeral, was apparent.

I found Vic's behavior annoying, and I became irritated as words formed in my mind. "Vic, I told you a long time ago that being dead might not be what you expected. If you'll notice, your sons aren't having as much fun as you are! As a matter of fact, they're pretty miserable, and the way you are behaving is really not proper." Of course, what would be proper under these circumstances wasn't clear, but I was pretty sure that laughter was out of line. I realized that I was nagging and finding fault with him in death just as I had in life, which didn't make me feel any better. After all, he was behaving like his usual self, showing little concern for anyone but himself.

The service ended and Vic was gone. I rose and followed my family to seats at graveside. I was still upset with him.

That was a long time ago, but the memory of our last visit is as real as was my watching my sons' grief. It happened. Why is it worth rehashing now? Maybe someone now will take a different view of death. Personally, I'm grateful to Vic that he helped me turn believing into knowing. It has made a tremendous difference in how I've since lived my life.

Just because we get out of a worn-out body, we do not suddenly turn saintly or into a righteous angel. As a matter of fact, we enter the next life at the same degree of advancement we had when we left our Earth life. Those of us who are given more time here can still work on character problems. I believe

I am a little less of a nag than I used to be; but more important, my witnessing Vic's presence at his own funeral confirmed my belief that death definitely did die.

Shirley Keeline

Going Home

Jean had always been a spiritual person. When I first met her in the late 1960s, we were working together in one of the many great restaurants on "restaurant row" in Los Angeles. I did not know about her special spirituality at that time. I did not even know about my own, for I was too busy making a living.

After several years of employment there, I left the restaurant to pursue another occupation. Jean and I kept in touch at Christmas, and spoke on the phone a number of times throughout the year. One day, I heard Jean that had had a stroke and was struggling to live.

Time passed, and in 1988 I received a call from her telling me that she had moved closer to my area. When I visited her a short while later, we had a great time talking and catching up with everything in our lives. In our many meetings that followed, Jean told me about the journey she was on and about the spiritual philosophies she believed in. I always wanted to hear more. Due to her stroke, Jean was handicapped and had fallen on hard times. She was forced to live in meager circumstances. City and federal agencies provided her money to live on and subsidized her housing. When she was told by these agencies that she was expected to resume working again in one to two years, she panicked. She felt she could never work again.

I offered to help her by taking her to interviews and in making phone inquiries. I suggested she find a job where she could sit, such as a computer operator. I told Jean that she could develop that skill during the next two years. But Jean was afraid of this new beginning. It was not long after that she developed an earache. She had no relief from the constant pain in her ear, and for several months the doctors could not find the cause of her illness. Then one day, the diagnosis came. It was cancer. It had already spread and there was no hope for her survival. Regardless, Jean was full of hope, and she said, "I will get well again."

Since she had been having a hard time swallowing her food for the last few weeks, I got her a blender, which allowed her to puree her food. But soon she was not eating very much and was losing weight. Rosi, our mutual friend, helped Jean realize that she had to go to a nursing home so she could be taken care of and get proper nourishment. Reluctantly, Jean agreed, and we made the arrangements. It was not easy to get this finalized, but Rosi and I were finally able to make her comfortable with the nursing home solution. In April 1990, with Jean's permission, we dissolved her small household and I packed all the things that were to be sent to her mother and sister, who lived in the Midwest.

It had been a little over a month since Jean had moved to the nursing home. I visited her often and she was always cheerful and never complained. On Thursday, May 31, 1990, I visited Jean again. The nurse told me that she had just given Jean a morphine injection, and she would be asleep soon.

When I walked into her room, I could not help but notice that her face was like fine porcelain, and the whites of her eyes were a pure white. Jean was beautiful! She spoke in a whisper, and said that she had seen the most beautiful light in her sleep, full of endless love. She knew that this light was going to take her home soon. When I held her hand and gently started to stroke her forehead, Jean said, "Oh, that feels so good, please don't stop. You have been such a good friend, Martha. Have a good life," and she drifted off to sleep. I knew when I left that this was the last time I would see her.

The following Sunday morning, Rosi called me and told me Jean had died. I was asked a week later to come to Jean's memorial service, which was to be conducted by her long-time spiritual teacher. What I discovered there was one of my first glimpses of proof that we live on after death, that we only leave our body behind, and that we are much more than we think.

It was a beautiful service. Rosi was present, and so were many of Jean's friends. The reverend spoke for a long time of Jean's life and how much he appreciated her as his pupil, and how many times she had challenged his teachings over the years. He was sad to see her leave having had only fifty-nine years of life. He said that he had been with Jean on the last day of her life, and that she had known she was leaving soon. Jean had told him she would give him a sign when she had left, and she asked him to contact her after her passing.

Later that night, the reverend was working on his Sunday sermon and was late going to bed. About one A.M., he woke up suddenly and saw a white light circulating in one corner of his bedroom. "Jean, you have gone," was his spontaneous remark, and after he prayed and sent love and light her way, the light slowly faded. Twenty minutes later, he received a call from the nursing home that Jean had passed on a short while earlier.

At Christmastime in the same year, I had a chance to speak with Rosi again. Since she was still a pupil of Jean's teacher, she had the opportunity to be present when the reverend attempted to contact Jean on the Other Side. "We heard Jean's voice," Rosi said. "She told us she was very, very happy and had no more pain. She was surrounded by many beautiful flowers and a little cat, and she lived in a very nice place. She was studying, and she just loved all of it."

I often think of Jean and the way she lived and the way she left us. For me, this was an inspiration, and I started to read intensely about spirituality, reincarnation, and the reasons we are here. I have since become firmly convinced that we are spiritual beings, and we are here to experience earthly life with all of its lessons. Our true life begins again in our real home with many of our loved ones, and we leave this Earth in a process we call "dying," but which in reality is a going home.

Martha M. Granda

Well, I'm Going Now!

My father, Marcus, reached his eightieth birthday in May 1989. He had been ill for some time. He was suffering from emphysema and lymphoma and was confined to bed at a nearby hospital. There he drifted in and out of consciousness during the last four weeks of his physical life.

The night before Marcus died, I visited him and found him very alert and wanting to chat. In fact, he asked me to buy him a newspaper so he could catch up on the news. He also asked me to get him a bottle of Blue Nun wine so he could give it to the nurses who had been so kind to him during his hospital stay.

When I returned with the newspaper and wine, Marcus began to recall many events from his youth and the good times we had enjoyed as I was growing up. His memory of these experiences spanning many decades was exceptional, considering he had been in and out of consciousness the previous month. I spent two hours with him, sharing these life experiences, then left him with words of love. I was feeling elated that Marcus was showing remarkable recovery and would soon be well enough to return home. But that was the last time I saw him alive.

The next morning while I was at work, Marcus returned to the semiconscious state, but was very peaceful when my mother, Joyce, and my daughter, Rennae, arrived at the hospital to visit him. The doctor told Mom that he felt Marcus did not have much time left, so Mom and Rennae sat quietly holding his hands. After a few minutes, he awoke, sat up in bed, smiled brightly while looking beyond the foot of the bed, and said in a clear voice, "Well, I am going now!" He then sank back onto the pillows and departed.

Although my mother was saddened to lose her husband of fifty-three years, she felt assured that he had been ready to go at that moment. She was particularly pleased that I had been able to spend such joyous time with him the night before.

Mom is still able to live by herself and prefers to be in her own home. She often tells me that she feels Dad's presence in the house, which gives her great reassurance and comfort in her advancing years. Even though she tells me that she is ready to go at any time, she is having too much fun to leave just yet.

Over the years, my wife and I have read many books about near-death experiences, angelic presence, reincarnation, and the spiritual domain. We are in total agreement with the truth that we are spiritual beings having a human experience, and not the other way around. Little wonder we were excited and encouraged when we came into contact with the book *The Messengers*, and have continued to enjoy the wonderful messages of love and support available to all of us in the monthly newsletters of The Great Tomorrow, our nonprofit foundation. Thank you for sharing the truth.

Marc Faulks

The Violets

Adenocarcinoma is what caused my mother's death. They said it had already metastasized, and that no surgery and no medication would help. How could that be? She was only sixty years old. Hadn't the Lord promised me that we would mend our relationship? Now it seemed too late.

My thoughts were spinning. Had I mistaken the voice of the Lord? No, I knew that voice. It was the same voice I had heard for almost thirty years. But I did not understand. I was so sure that Mom and I would one day talk and hug and that she would tell me that she loved me and that everything would be okay. I was so confused. What do I do, Lord? How do I endure all the regret? Why do I still feel that she is unsettled?

Although Mom had become a Christian and quit drinking a long time ago, maybe I was just remembering that haunting fear that was in her eyes those last few months. Maybe I was feeling uneasy because she refused to discuss the important things that needed to be discussed, even though she knew her disease was terminal. I don't know, I just don't know.

Months later, as my daughter Nichole and I walked by my mother's grave, I had those same perplexing thoughts. As I looked down at her grave marker, I heard Mom say, distinct as ever, "That's where they planted my body." What did she mean, "planted my body?" What an odd thing to say from one who was so timid and afraid. Was I mistaken? Did I think I heard something just then?

When I explained this odd occurrence to Nichole, she smiled and said, "Oh Mom, that sounds just like something Grandma would say. She probably thought she was just being funny." But it still did not seem quite right, and besides that, why would I hear something a dead person said?

Then what was happening? Was my brother also losing his mind? Maybe it was just an exaggerated style of the grieving process, but my brother swore Mom was still in the house and that Dad saw her too.

"She's been in the motor home and she is in the house too," Frank said. "I feel her presence. I know she is here."

"Sure Frank, sure," I thought as I hung up the phone.

All right, okay . . . then I knew that I needed to pray about this. It had gone too far. "Dear Lord, what is going on? Is this of you? Why is this happening? What is this unsettling feeling that I keep getting? Is Mom not with you?"

Waves of the witness of the Holy Sspirit suddenly enveloped my body. Next thing I knew, it was no longer Mom talking to me—I was talking to her. "Go towards the Light, Mom. Turn around and go towards the Light," I told her. Then in my mind's eye, I saw her do just that, and soon thereafter came a second confirmation from spirit, even stronger than the first.

So that was it! She had been so ill for so long that she was somehow too disoriented and confused after she left her body to follow the Light back home. That was why the odd comment at the cemetery and the sightings. All I could do was praise the Lord. She was in the spirit world now. She would be all right and I could leave this all behind me. Mom was with God and she was where she was supposed to be. Now I felt that sense of contentment and peace. Finally.

The weeks passed and no more voices came from beyond. However, I soon began to notice a fragrance around my home. It was the perfume of violets everywhere. Their aroma was like . . . Mom!

As I opened the door and walked into the bedroom, there it was again, except this time it was even stronger than before. I said to my husband, "Dear, come here and tell me what you smell."

"What is that fragrance? Smells like lilacs, or violets, or something like that. Where did it come from? We haven't been home all day," he replied.

"It's my mom. I just know it is," I said.

"What does this mean? What are we supposed to do?" he said, backing out of the room.

At the time, what it meant didn't matter to me. What did matter was that someone else could smell it too, and that I wasn't losing my mind. Besides, she was probably just saying, "Thank you." She came, she gave me a hug, and she filled the air with her fragrant violets.

After a few days had gone by I came to realize the full purpose of Mom's violets. Without uttering a word, we had finally discussed all of the important things. Even more importantly, I felt a deep sense of peace just knowing that our relationship was mended—precisely as God had promised.

Kimber Lea Allen

Our Final Good-bye

My Great-Gram's journey to God happened fourteen years ago, and that is when my experience with God began.

My Gram and I had been very close. We shared a special bond. She was such a lively gem. Gram could always make me laugh, even when she was in a great deal of pain herself. She had a beautiful smile.

My Gram and I couldn't always be together as we would have liked, as she lived in Arizona and I in Ohio, but that didn't stop our hearts from being connected to each other.

Then the day came. My grandmother called to tell us that they didn't expect Gram to make it through the night. I had known that this day was coming, but still I wasn't ready to let her go. She was such a big part of my life. It tore at my soul not to be able to be there with her, to be able to say, "I love you," and "Good-bye," for one last time. I didn't want to believe that I would never see or hear from her again. How wrong I was.

That night, I had an out-of-body experience. My soul traveled to be with my great-grandmother's soul. Gram was lying in her hospital bed, and I was at her side, holding her hand, letting her know that I was there with her. I don't remember any words being spoken; we were communicating through our thoughts. This time, I was able to say how much I loved her and that I would miss her.

That night, God sent His angels to guide my Great-Gram home. They came to her in a wonderfully brilliant light that started at the end of her bed. I saw them reaching out to her, and when I looked back down at her, I saw that she had also reached out to them and was ready to take the great journey beyond. As I stood there, I knew that I would see her again and that she would live on in my heart and memories.

As of today, my Gram periodically pays me a visit, either in my dreams when she wants to give me a message, or in my home. She lets me know she's around by leaving the scent of her perfume in the air. Not only am I able to smell it, but my family members can also. I know that this is living proof that love and the spirit are eternally one and never-ending.

Cathie L. Wells

I'm Here, Tilton, I'm Here

I have been a practical nurse for over twenty-six years and have comforted and eased the fears of many patients who were referred to as terminal. I have comforted many relatives and friends who were devastated by their losses. I have had to comfort the occasional fearful reactions of care-givers, nurses, and nursing aides who were fearful of approaching the dying or deceased. I want to tell you of two incidents that stand out in my career.

The first incident happened during the summer of 1988. I was working the seven A.M. to three P.M. shift. I had noticed that whenever I was within about one hundred yards of any resident or patient who had just passed, I could feel an out-rushing of some sort of energy. I usually kept that knowledge to myself, knowing how devastated those who were left behind were feeling. I know firsthand how it feels, because I lost my beloved grandmother to diabetes and a younger brother of fourteen years to a heart attack. My brother had been born with heart murmurs. He survived one heart oper-ation but did not make it through the second one.

I felt this outpouring of energy as an intense joy, like an explosion of energy bursting from people at the end of their chosen journey. I knew that my part in it was to make them feel as comfortable as possible, to do my utmost to calm them and be there for them, even if it meant holding a hand long after my shift was over or singing a hymn. Whatever it took to ease their anxiety, I knew I would do. Many very good, caring nurses and nurse's aides are still doing the same.

A lady on a floor other than mine was suffering terribly with metastasized cancer and brittle-bone disease. Both were a source of constant debilitating pain. The nurses were on a voluntary, round-the-clock, caregiving watch. They never left the poor lady alone for a moment, because her greatest fear was of being alone. A soothing voice and a warm comforting hand were always there for her. After being gently bathed at 8:40 A.M., she reached out to the young nurse's aide who was at her side. At 8:44 A.M., the lady breathed a deep sigh, and then the aide felt an explosion of gold-white energy and heard a kind of faraway shout of happiness from the lady. It scared the living daylights out of the girl, who screamed and ran straight to the nurses' station, stammering about a great light and a shout coming from the lady.

Shaking and deeply fearful, the girl would not go back in the room, so the floor nurses attended to the lady and called the doctor. I was downstairs at another unit but I felt the explosion of energy as a sensation of intense joy.

I thought to myself, "Someone has left their pain behind and jumped into the arms of the angels." Soon after, it was my break time and I spoke to the nurse's aide. How glad I was to calm her fears and help her realize that she was a direct witness to a rapture. How proud I was to see understanding and renewed courage fire up in her eyes. We are here to comfort the living and to do our best, just as she and the others had been doing, to see that every last pain and anxiety is comforted and eased to the best of our ability. How else can we continue to live with ourselves if we do not do our best? What the nurse's aide saw was the same lady she had taken care of, jumping with joy right into the angels' arms.

Is that anything to be afraid of? No! I might not have been there when my little brother passed, but after having seen and felt something many times like I have just described, I have no worries over what happened to him or how he is doing. I reminded the young aide that the first thing the angels always tell those they address in scripture is, "Fear not, be not afraid." So by calming the lady's fears all those weeks and long hours, we are following the same instructions of God as the angels. The nurse's aide reflected and realized there was nothing to fear. She was no longer afraid.

The second incident I want to relate involved one of the younger nurse's aides, a twenty-something mother of two small children. She was very slim and frail with a shy, lovely smile that all her co-workers would try to coax out of her. She had troubles at home, and soon after beginning work, she asked if she could take any replacement spots for people calling in sick because she was more than happy to come in at any time. I was the acting supervisor, and after arriving at the hospital, she would come up to me and let me know, "I'm here, Tilton, I'm here!" She struck quite a picture: her proud white starched uniform framed her fine, silky-black complexion. As she worked with the other aides, we had many chances to make her smile.

One night, she did not come in as scheduled. We all felt a terrible foreboding and dread. When the head nurse called her house, her distraught mother answered, saying that she had been on a short trip out of state to see some of her family and had been in an accident. The car that she had been in with her cousin had been hit on the passenger side by a drunk driver. She had been killed instantly. Everyone on staff at the nursing home was deeply upset. We took a collection to send to her family, and everyone went in shifts to the funeral.

Two weeks later, she was still very much in our thoughts and prayers. I had just come on shift and was looking at reports, settled into the night's paperwork after making rounds. The other nurse's aides were in pairs, changing and helping their patients. It was twelve-thirty A.M., the time that she used to come in to replace someone who'd called in sick. The others said that they thought they saw a slim, white-clad, black figure going past them down the hallway.

What did I see at the desk? When I looked up, there she was, dressed in her crisp white uniform, walking down the hallway towards me with that dazzling, brightly lit smile. She stopped about ten feet from me and I heard her voice, loud and clear, saying to me, "I'm here, Tilton, I'm here!" Then she vanished.

When I told the others what I had seen and heard, we all cried, even harder than when we first heard she had been killed. For some of us, it was a renewed sadness, but for most of us, it was awe and joy. But I have to tell you one thing: No one was fearful or afraid.

I can still almost hear her, even though I am no longer "Tilton" and it has been many years since her passing. The message she gave, "I'm here, Tilton, I'm here," still lives with me.

Susan Lee

My Best Friend

I knew it was going to be an emotional challenge for me in many ways when it came time for my dad to pass on. I loved him in every way. He was a very special, patient, funny, kind, and understanding father. We never hugged, kissed, or even said, "I love you," to each other, yet his love was always felt. There was never a moment when I had a thought that Dad might not love me.

Dad was eighty-six years old when he passed on in March of 1974. For the last four to six years of his life, he was living on love, his doctor said. Medically, my dad should have been dead, he added.

Within a month after Dad's passing, he visited me. I was in the bed with no lights on. I could see the light from the living room shining down the hall. My husband was watching television. I was eight months pregnant and our four-year-old daughter was fast asleep. Just minutes after I lay down, there was Dad at the foot of my bed. He looked like a hologram, full-size and in perfect colors. Dad looked exactly as he had in his physical life, sitting in his rocking chair. It frightened me beyond words.

Dad and the rocking chair were suspended about three feet off the floor. It scared me so that I ran down the hall to get my husband, but Dad was gone when we got back. A few weeks went by, and the same thing happened again.

Then a few months went by, and one night something awakened me. I checked on the girls, and they were fine.

Then for no reason, I went into the living room and looked out the window towards my mother's house next door. There was a bright moon that night. I saw Dad walking to Mom's house from ours. He looked exactly like he had in his physical life. He did not look like a hologram this time. Dad had a special light surrounding him that was different from anything I had ever seen before. He did not cast any shadows. About a month later, I again saw him in the same place outside at night. Both of these times, I felt overcome with emotion, but I was no longer frightened.

I now know that these sightings were intended to be wonderful moments for us to share together. Dad so desired to let me know that he was alive, but at the time, I did not understand. I haven't seen Dad since 1975, but he lets me know that he is present by the lights, telephone, and the smell of the tobacco that he used to chew.

Nobody believed me when I told them about these events, but I knew what I had seen and I still can see the entire scene in my mind's eye. I will love my special soul mate and friend forever, my very special Dad.

Bettie Whitehead

Princess

When I was six years old, my grandmother was my best friend. After school, I eagerly ran to her house to share the events of the day. She taught me how to be a good listener and a great storyteller, and how to laugh at life but not at people.

Suddenly, she became ill and was taken to the hospital. After four days, they allowed her to return home. It was very hard for me to be patient at school, for I could not wait to run home to be with her. We lived next door to my grandparents. As I approached the house, I noticed lots of cars, and thought to myself, how nice to have a welcome home party for my grandmother. That's when my mother came outside and told me that my grandmother had died just before she was to leave the hospital.

The next week was filled with the deep pain of grieving. Soon after, my grandfather started talking about how he was seeing and hearing my grandmother in the house. At first, I was scared, not knowing if something was wrong with him or if I might see a ghost.

I decided to talk with my grandfather about what he was experiencing, and he shared with me that Grandmother would come to him while he was lying in bed. If he didn't try to get up, she would stand lovingly beside his bed. He said he felt enormous unconditional love and peace from her. He could hear her thoughts in his head, for she didn't speak out loud. Grandfather said he was never afraid, but felt it was natural to see her and to hear her words in his head. Grandmother's visits offered him peace and frequently eased his pain of loss. He said he knew that she was in a beautiful place, and it took away his fear of death.

Since that conversation, I have felt my grandmother's presence at various times in my life, and I have changed my beliefs about death as being a final and sorrowful event to death being about a joyous experience in the cycle of life.

Now as an adult, during my nursing career, I have been present at many death experiences and have felt when a person's spirit disconnects and journeys on. I always feel peace and joy and say a blessing to the spirit. My nursing has also placed me in several positions to be present when patients returned from near-death experiences (NDE). Every patient who experienced an NDE said it tremendously changed their life. They spoke of being in a place with light and unconditional love, and how they didn't want to come back to this life of pain and conflict. I felt blessed to be present with these patients as they freely expressed what had happened to them.

Two years ago, Princess, my lovable female schnauzer, suddenly died. My male schnauzer and I missed her gentle spirit. One morning, two weeks after her death, I was lying quietly, reflecting on how special she was. Just then, my male dog jumped up on the bed and lay beside me. Eyes closed, I was petting him and talking about Princess. Suddenly, I felt her presence and felt her weight as she lay across my hip the way she used to. I was not asleep but fully awake. I still had my hand on my male dog, but I knew not to open my eyes. I just went ahead with my other hand and stroked my female dog's presence. Feeling her brought such peace to my spirit. I remembered what a clown she had been and I started to laugh rather than hold on to the pain and grief of losing her.

Several pet owners have shared similar stories with me. We agree that we have changed our thoughts on dying and think more of celebration than sorrow and grief.

When I attend funerals now, to the grieving family members I express thoughts of joy and celebration of the life of their deceased family member. I encourage them to feel this rather than sadness at their departure, because there is no such thing as death.

Cathy Paradise

As we leave the Earth plane for the spiritual world, we will enter the level of the spiritual world consistent with how high we have climbed the mountain, consistent with the level of our spiritual attainment on Earth.

—In God's Truth

The Apartment

My husband, children, and I moved to a new community and we soon discovered a family living next door who not only were delightful neighbors but also became good friends. Their children were older than our children and within a few years left their parents' home to start their adult lives.

Ellie and Bob, the couple who lived next door, and my husband and I would often spend evenings together over a game of bridge, or just visiting. As a pastime, Ellie and I would go on shopping expeditions.

One day, Ellie phoned with the sad news that Bob had died. I hurried next door and told Ellie I would help in any way I could. She needed help preparing for relatives who would be coming from out of town. Another neighbor and I readied the house for the expected guests and then we went home to prepare food for them.

At home, I was thinking of what food to prepare when suddenly standing in front of me was Bob. I was stunned. He said nothing, but gazed at me with calmness. I understood he was conveying the thought, "I am all right." I noticed he wore what looked like a brand new blue shirt, the same blue that Ellie and I had seen on our last shopping excursion. It seemed that Bob wanted me to tell Ellie he was all right.

I thought maybe Ellie would think I had imagined things if I told her I had seen her husband. But I had to tell her, it was too important not to. I went back to see Ellie. She listened quietly as I told her the story of seeing Bob. When I began to tell her about Bob wearing a new blue shirt, she gasped, "Bob just bought a new blue shirt. Come with me to the bedroom. It's in his chest of drawers." Ellie produced the blue shirt Bob had recently purchased. It was the same blue as the shirt he wore when appearing to me.

Shortly after this, Ellie moved to Indianapolis to live with her brother. They had begun apartment hunting when I had another spiritual experience with Bob. I was dreaming and found myself standing in a building's foyer. I glanced around. Directly ahead of me was a short flight of stairs leading to a landing. Bob stood on the landing looking at me, and as soon as he had my attention, he gestured toward a door at his left. I was given to understand this door led to the apartment where Ellie and her brother were to live. As far as I knew, Ellie and her brother had not yet found an apartment.

I decided to tell no one but my husband about this second experience with Bob. I wanted to think it through for myself. Was I hallucinating the whole thing? When I told my husband, I included all the details.

Weeks later, Ellie told us that she and her brother had signed a lease for an apartment in a building under construction.

A year later, my husband and I were invited to visit Ellie and her brother in Indianapolis. We drove to the city, found the address, and walked into the building where Ellie and her brother lived.

There it all was, exactly as Bob had shown me! I had told my husband all the details of the building. The inside entrance, the stairs, the landing, the railing around the landing, and the door leading into Ellie's apartment. I wasn't crazy! The experiences with Bob were authentic. Not only did I realize the validity of my experiences with Bob, but my husband knew the details as well as I did, because I had shared them with him often. Best of all was that we had proof that Bob lived in spirit and knew something of Ellie's future. Fantastic! Even now, I still wonder how Bob could show me where Ellie and her brother were going to live when the building hadn't even been built yet.

That Bob was involved in some way with his dear wife's life was evident. Life surely does continue after the graduation we call death, and so does the love between people.

Eva Jennings

The Envelope

Funerals were always depressing events in my life. That was until a few years back, when my grandfather died. He was a wonderful old Irishman by the name of Jim Dempsey. He was a dyed-in-the-wool Catholic with lots of character and a great sense of humor.

I lived with him for a time while I was attending cooking school. Once after I returned home, he entertained me with a story of his trip back from the grocery store earlier that evening, just after sunset. Apparently, two young hoodlums, as he described them, were following close behind him. About halfway home, he began to realize that the footsteps were getting closer and closer. Gramps was eighty-two years old and stood six feet tall and weighed 190 pounds. He said to me, "John, I just got tired of waiting for them to make the first move. I threw the groceries down, spun around with my fists in the air, and yelled, 'Come and get it, punks!'" With that, they took off in the other direction.

My parents would visit Jim regularly and take him to his favorite restaurant, Spenger's Fish Grotto, in Berkeley. The only condition was that over the years, they never let him pay for a meal, not once. Shortly before he died, he gave my mom an envelope with instructions to open it after he died and to read it before his funeral. My mom followed his instructions after his passing.

The letter inside the envelope read, "It's my turn to buy dinner. You are to use as much money from my account as you need and invite everyone who wishes to come to dinner after the funeral." My mom thoroughly enjoyed telling us kids and a number of friends about my grandfather's wish. Gramps was finally getting even with my parents for never allowing him to buy dinner.

About fifty of us gathered at the bar waiting for our dining room at the restaurant to be set up. We toasted Jim with Guinness Stout and Jameson's Irish whiskey. The evening began slowly with one funny story about Gramps, then another. Before the evening was over, I'll bet we heard close to one hundred stories about my grandfather and his life. One minute we were crying, and the next we were howling with laughter.

That's the part I loved the most and will never forget— all those wonderful stories from so many different people. I remember driving home from that dinner feeling wonderful and very upbeat. It was one of the best parties I had ever been to and here it was, a funeral. I guess you could call it an old-fashioned Irish wake.

Now whenever I attend a funeral reception, I get together with a small group and begin telling stories about the person's life. Soon after, everyone in the group has to tell their special story about the person who has passed. Before you know it, people are laughing through their tears and recalling heartwarming stories of a soul's journey through life. Then out of the corner of my eye, I see Gramps smiling and I know I am carrying on a wonderful old tradition.

John Lincoln

Sweetest Sister

When I was seventeen, my fifteen-year-old sister died of brain cancer. Much of this time is a blur for me (I am now forty-one), but the most vivid moment was when, minutes after she died, I walked into her room and her spirit had already lifted from her body, but she was waiting for me. She quietly said, "It's okay, Abbie. It's okay."

In the following years, she has come to visit me a few times, not with words but with her presence, which has been near my right shoulder. This has been very comforting to me. I have held tight to these experiences, but have also dealt with a lot of faith during times of crisis.

Now, after reading your books and monthly newsletter, I feel I am returning to my own spirit, to that part of me that really heard my sister tell me that it was and is okay. I feel that it truly is okay to pass on, and I believe in the work our spirits are needing to do in order to be closer to God. I believe that this process we go through in grief is an important part of our human condition, which we do not understand but we experience in order for our spirits to grow. Not a day has gone by that I don't miss my sister. In our human condition, we need each other's physical presence to help and understand each other. We also need the spirits who touch us in so many ways.

Didn't Jesus feel great grief when Lazarus died? I believe that He understands, too. That, to me, is the greatest gift that God has given us. His son understands and supports us in our human journey and encourages the spirits and angels to help us and guide us close to Him. Of this, I am sure.

Abbie Reiquam Nelson

The Vision

Do our loved ones present themselves in recognizable form after they make their transition? The following is an account of the vision I saw of my former husband Charles on an evening in the spring of 1993.

As background, allow me to acquaint you with Charles. He was known to many as the "gentle giant." Soft-spoken, kind, nurturing, always ready to listen, he stood six feet eight inches tall, his back straight and erect at seventy-two years of age. His movements were slow and deliberate. His manner was calm and gentle. When he was angry, his green-blue eyes turned steel-gray, his only visible sign of emotion. He was a very controlled man. Some considered him handsome, his facial features being without irregularities. His large body was perfectly proportioned from head to toe. He had iron-gray hair. Though he had a slight paunch when I met him in 1988, he was skeletal when he left this world.

It was a pleasant sunny day in January 1993 when his transition took place, by his own hand, when he pressed a gun into the roof of his mouth and pulled the trigger.

Finding his body in the back shed was a horror for me, though mercifully, I saw only a portion of him. Charles would not have considered this suicide, and in a larger sense, neither did I. We had four loving years together—a union and communication of inner spirit allowing for a rapport not generally shared by most couples. Our talks on metaphysical subjects and about what happens on the other side of the veil were frequent. Charles had no fear of death. To him, it was simply a renewal of his continuing life, only in another form.

His sickness began in the fall of 1991. He loved life and our life together. He didn't want to leave me. He was in and out of the Marion Community Hospital several times. During his last sojourn there, he described to me the times, both day and night, when the angels would shake his feet— they extended way beyond the bottom of the bed—and say, "Come on, it's time to come with us." He'd respond by saying, "I can't leave Maggie." This large, oversized man would weep, tears glistening on his cheeks every time he related these experiences.

Charles's pain was great, nearly unbearable, increasing each month as the cancer invaded his spinal column, then his intestines, then squeezing against his heart. He had only a little time left. He knew where he was going; the transition to the other side of life was a release, a separation from his painful body. It meant a reunion with his beloved mother. He didn't want to leave me, but he hated to stay and be the physical burden he knew he was.

My grief was like a golden light as well as a hole of pain. I understood and accepted his passing over. I got on with my life, knowing this was his wish for me.

The activities I busied myself with did not interfere with my memories of our happy days together. The main negative experience for me was the recurring replay in my mind of finding his body. Many nights, I would awake and see it all again.

As spring brought fresh green leaves to the trees and colorful flowers sprouting in the landscape, I continued to renew my own life. I had formed a habit of propping myself up in bed with pillows of all sizes. I'd turn on the television and watch a movie or read a book, sometimes doing both. This particular evening in April 1993, I was watching a movie that was dull and uninteresting. I found myself only half listening, still conscious, but drifting in and out of reverie. My thoughts were not about Charles or anything reminding me of him.

I glanced down at the foot of the bed, and there to the right was a vision of a table or desk, and seated in front of it was a plump woman with dark brown, shoulder-length hair, her back to me. Then my eyes moved further to the right and there was Charles, standing, filling up the doorway.

My immediate reaction was, "Oh, how tall he still is." He wore a white shirt, open at the throat, a shirt I'd seen him wear many times. His facial features were the same as in life, but his expression was wonderfully and marvelously changed. His countenance will always remain a vivid memory to me. A shining glow of supreme happiness and peace was reflected in every area of his face, forehead, cheeks, and chin, all of which expressed serenity and joy. A half smile tugged at the corners of his mouth, his lips slightly parted in gladness and wonder. His eyes were like jewels, glittering like stars. He was looking straight ahead in wonderment and contentment at the splendor and magnificence of Heaven. Then the vision faded and he was gone.

Charles had returned briefly in his earlier form to comfort me, to tell me that the transition to the Other Side was as we both had envisioned. Heaven was beautiful beyond anything found on the Earth. His vision came to tell me to not think of his physical passing, but to see him as a new creature in God's kingdom, at peace, sublimely happy. I will remember always this vision. I have no idea who the plump woman was. However, I no longer have the nightly frightening episodes of seeing Charles as I last saw him when he left this Earth.

Maggie Degear

Rob's Return

One evening in April 1977, I received a call from my sister Elinor with the staggering, tragic news of a plane crash in which my brother, Robert M. Furniss, and his wife, Sally, were passengers. It was a flight heading for Atlanta, Georgia, where they were scheduled to change flights and head home to Virginia Beach, Virginia.

The flight had encountered a terrible thunderstorm outside of Atlanta, and the plane lost first one engine and then the second. Amazingly, the pilot and co-pilot were able to land the plane on a road, but one wing struck a telephone pole, spinning the plane onto its side and causing it to burst into flames.

The airline was not releasing a list of survivors yet, but it was believed that Sally had been sent to the hospital, and perhaps Rob as well. This information was coming from Rob's law firm. None of us had even been aware that he and Sally had gone out of town.

God had given me the gift of being able to tune in to people's feelings. Quickly, I tuned in to Rob and recognized that he felt like the cat that had just swallowed the canary. He was happy and was amazed.

I reported this to Elinor, and we cheered in great relief. Poor Sally, on the other hand, was extremely strained and in terrible pain. Then it hit me. Could Rob feel like the cat that ate the canary because his body had not made it and he was dead? He had seemed very much alive and well. It was an awful, downhearted thought for us, but very possibly a true one.

My teenage children had heard my end of the phone conversation and had seen the crash site on the television. In horror, we had watched huge flames engulf the plane.

Repeatedly, I tuned in to Rob that night, each time seeing that saucy, cocky, bigger-than-life expression on his face. Being under a great deal of stress myself, I found it impossible to trust or accept any of my own feelings. Most certainly, I could not accept his being gone, no matter how pleased he appeared.

Soon, we heard that Sally was severely burned, and that she was out of her mind with pain and refusing to take medication until they told her whether Rob had made it. The hospital insisted again that such information had to come from the airline and that they were not allowed to give it out. Sally carried on until finally they told her, stating the news was unofficial that Rob had not made it. His body was there in the same hospital, dead upon arrival.

Rob was fifty-two, a grand person. We still thought of him as a fun-loving young attorney. Having co-founded the law firm of Furniss & Davis in Norfolk, Virginia, he had been an extremely ethical attorney. I was six years younger, the baby of the family, and regardless of my age, Rob had always introduced me as his baby sister.

It was forever and a year, seemingly, before the airline released the bodies. For myself, it was one of the hardest, most painful times of my life. Knowing Rob was alive and well in spirit was wonderful, but giving him up wouldn't work for me yet. Finally, we received the coroner's report. Rob had died before hitting the ground. He did not die from the collision, as one would imagine; he simply died before the plane crashed. The coroner couldn't explain this, but he said he had seen it before in plane crashes.

For the time we had to be in Virginia Beach for the funeral, we had been invited to stay with one of Rob's kind neighbors. Early in the morning, I was lying half-conscious in bed, aware of the birds singing as I realized this was the day of Rob's funeral. Every waking day since his death, my first conscious thought had been met with the awful, sharp pain of facing a dark, empty world without Rob. This day was no exception.

Usually, right after brief prayers for him, I'd tune in to Rob and find him still feeling great happiness, and smiling from ear to ear. But when I awoke that morning, suddenly, there he was! He was lying on a cot in front of me, as though we were back in our cottage at the beach where we had spent our long summers in childhood. He was lying on his side facing me, holding his head up by his perched arm, which was resting on his elbow. He was beaming at me, filling me with love, and without any words, conveying how happy and fulfilled he was, how he wanted me to share this bliss with him. I looked into those blue eyes, beaming back at him, thrilled beyond words.

He looked younger, probably around forty. I was not fully awake, yet I was still hearing the birds, and I knew without a doubt I was seeing Rob and sharing his bliss. Earlier when I tuned in to his feelings, I had felt his happiness and bliss; but seeing him and feeling his strong, loving presence was a million times better. Nonetheless, I still missed him so much, and for many weeks, waking up in the mornings and facing life without him was hard.

During this time, I was employed at the Sheraton Hotel in Reston, Virginia. I returned to work only a couple of days after his death, and I did pretty well emotionally. In the past, one of Rob's little tricks, one that nearly always knocked me off of my feet, had been to come up behind me and wrap his arms around my waist and lean his head down on my shoulder affectionately. My being on the job made no difference to him. He had such a strong presence, I was always aware of him approaching me, and believe me, I braced myself. I could be in the middle of a conversation with a customer, and then would try very hard not to show any reaction to this brother of mine. It was so funny, yet touched my heart so dearly, because he had done this many times before his death, and now even though he was gone, he was doing it!

The humor of this situation helped me to release the pain. I still miss him, and I will always wish we could chat about the gardens or whatever, but my heart doesn't have that terrible ache.

I have seen Rob in my dreams several times since his death, and I have been aware of his presence with me many times as well. We can still be close even though he is in the spiritual world, because I know that Rob is still with me. I have known this since the day of the plane crash, because for me, that was the day that death died.

Barbara Furniss Bauer

There are so many opportunities that are available to help others, but, in doing so, you also help yourself. You can become a messenger of God and nurture your soul. Your own spirit will become a manifestation of God.
—In God's Truth

Dearest Jim

A friend of mine was explaining to a few of us what a wonderful spiritual experience she was having walking a friend of hers through her death. I remember praying that I might have a similar experience and enjoy the personal growth from that experience. I certainly did not anticipate that the experience would turn out this way, as follows.

After twenty-nine years of marriage, I made a decision to move out on my own. Two years after I left my husband, Jim fell and hit his head. I remember picking up his hand and feeling there wasn't any life in it. Our children talked him into going to the doctor. He finally made an appointment, and my daughters and I went with him. X-rays were taken, and Jim and I waited in an office until the doctor gave us the diagnosis. The doctor announced that Jim had lung cancer. It left us all in total shock. We sat there in stunned silence, embracing. I was crying, but Jim had an accepting look on his face.

Jim's one wish was that I remarry him, which I did. He received radiation therapy for approximately four weeks, slowly getting weaker and weaker. His behavior was becoming ever more strange and unpredictable. On one occasion, when I took a day off, I left our daughter and son-in-law in charge of him. They became frightened and during this visit called 911. A helicopter, fire truck, several police cars, and an ambulance were dispatched.

Jim went peacefully to the hospital, where he was diagnosed as psychotic. He was sent to the psychiatric ward at the best hospital in town. Before long, he started having convulsions and was rushed to the intensive care unit, where they discovered the cancer had spread to his brain.

We held on to hope until the next day, when the doctors informed us that the tumors were multiplying rapidly. We made the heart-wrenching decision to take him off life support and let him pass on peacefully. The doctors, nurses, and attendants were wonderful, giving him loving care, explaining things to us and being very kind. We watched over Jim for three days, as family and friends kept coming and going. On the third day, while his family and friends were gathered, Jim took a deep breath and we felt his spirit leaving him. As this was happening, his sister began speaking in tongues. Jim's passing was beautiful, peaceful, the way dying is supposed to be.

At that point, the Priest took over. Honoring my husband's request to be buried at sea, he did some research and found it was possible and proceeded with the plans. Three separate times he needed to find a bigger boat to accommodate all the family and friends who wanted to participate. The boat was required to go out five miles from shore. The sea was very rough that day, and many on the boat became ill. I am sure Jim was amused at the sight. The casket was heavy, for it had to be weighted down so it would sink.

Over the next months, when I was alone, struggling with my grief, sometimes the lamp by my bed would come on by itself. I would then feel Jim's presence and comforting reassurance that in truth I wasn't alone. It has now been six years since Jim's passing and I am living in a larger home. Sometimes lamps in three different rooms come on by themselves, and it reminds me that I am never alone on this journey. I know that Jim's spirit is still with me, for death does not separate us from our loved ones.

Judy Wallace

The Divine Love

Even though money-wise I am not well-to-do, I am blessed with a lot of other things. As a matter of fact, I never took money seriously enough. My attitude was, "The servant need not worry about his daily bread."

Because I was born and brought up in India and am a Syrian Orthodox Christian living in the South, I received many opportunities in the state of Kerala to understand all the religious teachings. Beginning in primary school, religious teachings were part of every day's language class, which also included many stories of the different religious teachers such as Jesus, Muhammad, and Buddha.

According to Hindu religion, our life on this planet is a result of our previous karma, desire, and choice. Until we completely cease the desire and achieve the karma, we will continue returning. After liberation, we may also come back for a special mission.

A few years ago, I read a true story about something that happened to a young man who was working in a school about a hundred miles away from Kerala about fifteen years ago. His father died when he was a schoolboy and his grandfather brought him up. They were poor people, and when he finished college, he applied for jobs at many places. After a year or so passed, the young man finally got a job three hundred miles away in a village. Since he was very attached to his grandpa, whose health was not good, he had never traveled very much and had never stayed away from home, so he did not want to leave home for the job. His grandpa told him that he must take the job so that he could support the family, that it was the right thing to do. Finally, he accepted the job.

One evening, as he was going to bed to go to sleep, the young man saw someone standing at the door. It was almost dark and he looked carefully. He saw it was his grandpa, in good health and smiling. Without being aware of what was happening, he asked with surprise, "Grandpa . . . you're here?" His grandfather replied with a smile, "I just wanted to see you before I leave," and then he disappeared. The young man was not sure what had happened. With many thoughts in his mind, he went to sleep thinking that the next day, he should take a week's vacation and go home.

There was no telephone communication in this village like there is now, otherwise he would have called home. The next morning, he received a telegram from home that his grandpa had died the previous night. Later, he found out that the time he saw his grandpa was approximately the time of his death. There was no more than a twenty-minute difference.

For Hindus, it would be the most absurd belief to think we have only one life to live. It is unscientific. You cannot believe without an understanding, and if you do not understand, it is not necessary to believe it.

Scientifically speaking, nothing is created or is destroyed. If one has a strong desire to learn and understand, one will be guided to the destination. We go where we choose to go.

The Vedic scripture Isa Upanishad begins with these words.

AUM
Purnamadah
Purnamidam
Pumat purnamudachyate
Purnasya purnamadaya
Purnameva vashishyate

Translation:

That is the whole.
This is the whole.
From wholeness emerges wholeness.
Wholeness coming from wholeness,
wholeness still remains.

And Rajnesh had the following to say. Is it not beautiful!

The emphasis of the Upanishads is on wholeness. Remember, it is not on perfection but on wholeness. The moment one becomes interested in being perfect, the ego enters in. The ego is a perfectionist. The desire of the ego is to be perfect, and perfection drives humanity towards insanity.

At the heart of this phenomenal world, within all its changing forms, dwells the unchanging Lord. So, go beyond the changing and enjoy the inner. Cease to take for yourself what to others are riches. Continue to act in the world, for one may aspire to be one hundred.

Thus, and only thus, can a man be free from the binding influence of action (karma). Unillumined indeed are those worlds clouded by the blinding darkness of ignorance. Into this death sink all those who slay the Self.

Alexander Pollayil

The Visit

I am the mother of three boys and an artist. My family and I recently moved back to the United States after living in Hong Kong and Shanghai for several years.

Eleven years ago, on April 21, 1988, I had a spiritual experience that changed my life. I was in labor with my first child and Jesus appeared to me. He seemed to fill my consciousness, radiating love, forgiveness, and acceptance. He wore a white robe, and there was bright light all around Him. I sensed a humming sound as if from an energy source. There was a sense of joy and humor. I felt perfectly loved and worthy of His love.

After our son was born, I told my husband, "Jesus was sitting next to me." For a few years, however, I seldom thought of the experience and at times even doubted that it happened. Then, when I began a spiritual quest, seeking answers about life and wanting to understand my relationship with God, I realized that the experience had been real.

The image of Jesus and the love I felt remain vivid in my memory and assure me of my spiritual identity. As I grow in the knowledge of God's love for me and each of His children, the experience becomes more meaningful. Just as Jesus' life is spiritual and eternal, our lives are spiritual and eternal because we are all part of God and surrounded by God's love.

Marriott Little Sheldon

Aunt Margie, Dad, and Liz

I was about seven years old when my Aunt Margie died. I had always felt close to her even though I lived in Chicago and she lived in Florida. I saw her only once, when she came to visit us, but I think part of my special bond with her was that she had named me. Aunt Margie had two sons, and I always felt I should have been her daughter. She and my mom were very close. My mom had had to finish raising Margie and herself because their mom died when they were both young teenagers. Aunt Margie looked like my mom, except my mom is brunette and Aunt Margie was a blond. Aunt Margie died at thirty-five, when her heart gave out. She had always had a bad heart. My mom flew from Chicago to Florida for the funeral. That was the first death that I remember. It hurt to see my mom so upset, and I wished I could have helped her.

Mom kept her pain locked up, and there seemed to be an invisible wall around her. I think she didn't want to upset the six of us kids. I am the second-oldest, with one sister ten years older than I. When my mom came back from the funeral, she brought with her some of Aunt Margie's things. Among them were a bottle of perfume named Heaven Scent and a sheer white robe with puffy sleeves. I would get these things and spray on the perfume and put on the robe. I would then get my brother to ride me on the back of his tricycle just as fast as he could go so the robe would billow out behind me. That was so I could look just like Aunt Margie. I could literally see her flying alongside of us. I went through the same routine every time I wanted her to come play with us. She always seemed very happy and was always smiling.

Later, my mom had a painting done of Aunt Margie in which the artist used a photograph to get her likeness. However, she had the artist paint Aunt Margie wearing something different than what she had on in the photograph. When Mom brought the painting home, Aunt Margie was wearing the white fluffy dress that I saw her in when she would fly with me. Later as a teenager, when I would become upset or depressed, as so many teenagers do, I would see Aunt Margie lift off the painting. She would float away from the painting and be in the room with me and just smile. Then I would know that everything would be okay.

Also when I was a teenager, I shared a bedroom with two of my sisters. They had bunk beds while I had a twin bed on the other side of the room. We were always leaving the phone on the floor. One night, I heard something hit the phone, causing it to make a ringing sound. As I opened my eyes to see what it was, I could see that my younger sister Liz, who was on the bottom bunk, had woken up and was looking. We looked toward the phone and saw two pink slippers walking away. There was nobody in them, just the slippers. Liz looked scared, and I told her not to worry. "It's just Aunt Margie," I said to her. We went back to sleep.

In the morning, Liz did not believe me about it being Aunt Margie. I told her to ask Mother if Aunt Margie ever had slippers like the ones we saw. We went to my mom and Liz asked her. We did not tell Mom why we were asking.

She told us that Aunt Margie had been buried in a gown and pink slippers as we had described. She wanted to know why we were asking. We told her, but she did not believe us. I think she always thought I was a little weird. I would try to tell her about these things, and she would just say, "Oh, Cheryl," with a kind of exasperation that let me know she didn't believe anything I told her. My mom believes that once you die, that's it, there is nothing more. I keep telling her she's wrong. She will see one day.

There are many instances after this, but I am going to jump ahead to 1988, when my father died. I was thirty-four and living with my husband and three children. My parents were divorced, and my father lived in Beaumont, Texas, while his closest relatives, two brothers, lived in Houston.

Daddy had a bad heart and a few years earlier had had surgery on his heart at the VA Hospital. His physical health declined. He was in so much pain, he often talked of suicide as a way out, but this was against his beliefs. He was sure he wouldn't go to heaven if he committed suicide. As much as he wanted to die, he could not take his own life. My father was an overbearing, abusive man, an alcoholic who quit the bottle and took up the Bible.

I think that was worse. He believed that since the man was the head of the household, as Christ is head of the Church, and as people are supposed to "fear" God, this gave him the authority to be physically abusive. And he did this with a passion. None of my brothers and sisters would have anything to do with my father with the exception of Liz. She would put up with him when he came to visit, but it was always exhausting for her. My youngest brother Mike tried to have a relationship with him, but it wasn't a good one. I did not like my father, but I did love him.

One night, I got a call from Liz's husband that my father had had a massive heart attack and was in the VA Hospital in Houston. His heart had stopped, and it took them a while to get it going again. His brain had gone without oxygen for quite some time. He was hooked up to life support and in a coma. I knew my father would not want to be kept alive by machines. I could feel him as if he were going through a door and his clothing got caught on something and he couldn't pull free to move through the door.

Mike and I agreed to have life support turned off. Meanwhile, I called the VA Hospital and talked to my father's doctor. She recorded my instructions to turn off the life support and said she would call when it was over, because I could not travel to Houston at this time. My father had made Liz and me both promise him that when he died, we would not have a funeral and we were not to fly to Texas. He said our families needed the money more than we needed to have a funeral. After my talk with his doctor, I was feeling pretty bad. I sat outside looking at the night sky, and I wished I could hug my father one more time.

At that moment, I felt a warm hug from behind me. No one was there. At that instant, my husband came to the door and said the doctor was on the phone. She said my father had just died and my brother had not made it to Houston yet. I went back outside, crying and hoping I had done the right thing. I asked out loud if I could please be given a sign if I had done the right thing. Suddenly, a large shooting star flanked by two smaller ones on either side flashed across the sky. I took that as my sign, and I was amazed at the sight.

Many months later, I saw my dad in a dream. I am sure I was in spirit and not just dreaming. (I do this a lot and have become aware of the difference.) I was walking into a school classroom. All the children were sitting at their desks and they looked to be about ten years old. The teacher introduced me as a visitor and started to call roll. Then I realized that my dad was sitting in the middle of the classroom. All six feet two inches and 220 pounds of him were crammed into a student's desk. He had a serious look on his face. When his name was called, it was not the name he had in this lifetime. He did not recognize me. I realized he was in a place to learn, or rather to relearn. His memory seemed to have been erased. "Just as well," I thought. He did not need to carry the guilt of his actions into the next world. Although some feel he should have to pay for his actions, I would much rather he be taught from scratch so he could move forward. I never saw my dad again after this.

In 1995, Liz passed away in her sleep. She was only thirty-five years old. She had told me she knew she was going to die because she was just so very tired. She spent her last few days preparing, getting everything ready so she could leave. She called me and asked for a favor should she die. I am a wildlife rehabilitator and mostly raise squirrels. She had a squirrel she had raised with my help. Liz lived outside of Baton Rouge, Louisiana, and I still live in Atlanta, but she wanted me to bring her squirrel back with me to be released in a safe place, since there were so many hunters where she lived. I promised her that should anything happen to her, I would bring her squirrel back to Georgia to be released in the wild.

Thirty-six hours after I made my promise to her, Liz died. She passed peacefully in her sleep thirty minutes after going to bed. The autopsy could find no cause of death and it was ruled "natural causes." Of course, she did not tell anyone else she knew she was going to die. Once again, my poor mom was beside herself and I had no way to comfort her. Again it was, "Oh, Cheryl." I know I just upset my mom when I tell her what is going on, but I keep trying to help her. Anyway, my sister left behind two teenage boys, one husband, and one ex-husband, all of whom loved her very much.

Three months after her death, I was once again in spirit. This time, I found myself entering a very large white building. I was thinking it must be a Hilton. The building was on a lush green rolling hill. I went through the front doors into a foyer with rounded walls. I felt I was standing between two large pillars; looking ahead of me, I could see into what I thought was the lobby. The floor looked to be of green marble. In front of me was a crystal atrium that seemed to rise without end into the air. Crystal was on three sides, and the fourth side was a tall, skinny mountain with a waterfall that fell about a thousand feet. Birds of all sorts and butterflies were flying around. There was a beautiful light, although I could not see its source.

I then found myself walking into a hallway. There were doors all along the hallway going into separate rooms. Everything was white. "Nothing interesting here," I said out loud, and then stepped into an elevator. I went up to the third floor, and when the doors opened, the view was different. It was still a hallway with doors to separate rooms, but the doors had a rich, dark wood finish. The finish was polished so brightly that light reflected off it. The walls also had a polished wood finish and looked to be a dark walnut, with heavy wood trim. All the doorknobs and hardware were brightly polished gold.

The place was beautiful. I opened one of the doors, and inside were several women and a lot of babies in cribs. Some of the women were holding babies, and there was a lot of movement going on. Someone came up behind me and walked past me into the room. As I looked back over my shoulder to see who it was, I saw Liz. She smiled a beautiful big smile and entered the room carrying a sleeping baby. She laid the baby in a crib and picked up another baby who was awake. She sat down in a big green rocking chair and started rocking the baby to sleep. She never spoke to me; she only smiled. The other women spoke to me. One wanted to know if I knew how to put a hole in a nipple. She held a baby bottle up in front of me. I took it from her and fixed the nipple for her. I knew that these women weren't the babies' mothers.

A woman rushed up to me very upset, saying it wasn't her time. It was all the doctor's fault. I asked her who her doctor was and she said, "Dr. Moon." That was the doctor who had delivered two of my children. I assured her that Dr. Moon was a good doctor and I was sure it wasn't his fault. She calmed down and walked away. I saw her pick up a baby herself. Then I was outside the building. A woman dressed in white came out walking quickly carrying a baby. She looked up at me and said, "This one is from Chicago."

Later, I told my older sister Gwen about this. She asked about the baby from Chicago. I hadn't made the connection, but thirty years earlier, Gwen had lost one of her twin babies to crib death. They had lived in Chicago at the time. I took this part to be a message for her.

There have been many other instances in which I have been assured of the continuation of life after death.

Cheryl Noland

A miracle is defined as the intervention of God in your life. I have come to realize that angels are the messengers of God, and that angelic intervention in your life is truly a miracle.　　　　　　　　　—In God's Truth

I Know You're with Me, Doug

A very dear and close friend of mine, Doug Olson, died the day after Thanksgiving 1998. A diabetic, he had told me that summer he was "living on borrowed time." I did not want to believe it, but something inside said it was so.

Doug was taken to the local hospital a few days before Thanksgiving. By the time I got there, he was unconscious and hooked up to tubes, monitors, and a respirator. I visited him daily, but the news from the doctors was not encouraging. I spent some time alone with him and I knew he could hear me, even if his body could not. I told him I would like him to stick around, but I also knew that if it was his time, he could go. I told him I loved him, that he was my best friend, and that if he decided to leave, to look me up when he got back to this life. He died at 2:30 on Friday morning.

I awoke at around that time and felt certain that he had passed over. His daughter called shortly afterward to tell me that he had gone. A day or so later, Doug visited me. I saw nothing, I heard no spoken word, I just knew he was there. I felt his presence, sensed his thoughts, and knew he was laughing. We had a chance to say our good-byes.

I speak to Doug every now and then and know in my heart that he is always by my side. I miss his bodily presence and the many hours we spent in his kitchen over coffee or soda. He told the greatest stories, and we had wonderful discussions. I miss that and often tell him. I know he is still here. The stories aren't out loud like they used to be. Instead, I know them in my heart.

Mark A. Kruchowsky

Understanding

To understand death, we must understand the spiritual world. To understand the spiritual world, we must understand life.

While living in our mortal bodies, we are in truth a duality. We are immortal, but with a physical body that is not infinite. Our physical body had a beginning, its birth, and it has an end, its death. But in addition to our physical body, we have our spirit. It is a part of God, eternal and immortal, a part of the Source. It existed before the birth of our physical body and continues after the ending of our physical body.

Both our physical body and our spirit are presented to others through our mind. We are mind. Our mind is a reflection of what we feel, what we think, and of our decision making. Others relate to us and respond to us based on the manifestation of our minds, which reflects our personality and our value systems.

But our minds are governed by two separate influences. Those two influences are ego and spirit. Our ego comes from the material, mortal world. Our spirit comes from God and is a part of the spirit world. In most cases, they are competing with one another.

When someone does something wonderful and you are envious and jealous of that person, your mind has been influenced by your ego. If instead you feel admiration for that person, you have been influenced by your spirit, that part of God that resides within you.

When someone does something that causes you hatred, you are influenced by ego. But when someone commits an act against you and you feel forgiveness, your mind is being influenced by spirit. When someone close to you asks you for charity and you are capable of helping, but you refuse to help, your mind is influenced by greed, which is a manifestation of the ego. But should you instead act with generosity towards that person, your mind has been influenced by your spirit.

In all the choices we make in life, our ego and spirit are in constant competition and conflict. Do we lie or tell the truth? Do we deceive another so we may personally benefit, or do we act in honor? Do we discourage another, or do we offer them inspiration? Do we influence another by fear, or by offering them love? Do we view the misfortunes of others with indifference, or do we feel compassion? Each one of us has the ability to make the choice to live without this conflict by manifesting our spiritual mind rather than our ego.

I have often said in my lectures and writings that we are all on a journey to become one with that part of God that is inside of every one of us. What does that mean? It means that our minds would be exclusively influenced by spirit rather than by our ego. It means that we are manifesting God's will through the influence of that part of us that is God, rather than by our ego, which is almost always in opposition to our spirit.

What does this have to do with death? It is important to understand that our minds are everlasting, our minds are perpetual. When we shed our mortal bodies, our minds are no longer influenced by ego, for ego is left behind, just as surely as we have left our physical bodies behind. Instead, we are now influenced exclusively by spirit. When we are no longer in body, but instead in pure spirit, our minds also are pure spirit. We have no thoughts or desires to deceive, to cheat, to lie, to feel anger, hatred, prejudice, bigotry, selfishness, or greed. Instead, our thoughts are filled only with love and compassion to others.

Our goal in our journey in life is to have our spirit conquer ego while we are still in our body. Then it will no longer require death for us to be at one with God. We would be at one with the spirit of God that resides within us, because then our mortal minds and our spiritual minds will be one and the same.

In history, there have been individuals who succeeded in the challenge and had victory of the spirit over the ego, and who became manifestations of pure love and compassion. I refer to Jesus, Buddha, Siddhartha, Krishna, and Meher Baba. To a lesser degree but still obvious to the world, individuals who have also achieved this were Socrates, Pythagoras, Saint Thomas Aquinas, Saint Francis, and more recently, Mahatma Gandhi and Mother Teresa.

During your lifetime, if you are able to achieve having your mind become the manifestation of your spirit rather than your ego, surely that will be the day that death dies, for you shall be on Earth as you are in the spiritual world.

Nick Bunick

Part Two

Angels

Prior to January 14, 1995, I did not believe in angels. I thought angels belonged in the same toy box as the Tooth Fairy and the Easter Bunny. But on that day, I found out I was wrong. It was on that Saturday afternoon that I had the first of many, many angelic experiences.

Most of us, at one time or another, have read stories of people who supposedly had angelic encounters. But rarely did these people have a witness. Because of this, we do not know if their experiences were real or imagined.

The following stories are filled with love and joy, and in many cases, they had many witnesses in addition to the person who had the experience. These stories are for you to appreciate that, indeed, angels are the messengers of God and do intervene in our lives. These stories of angelic encounters surrounding the passing over of the spirit are filled with love and sensitivity, and will help us to understand the many different roles that angels play in our lives.

Nick Bunick

The word "angels" comes from the Aramaic word meaning messengers. The angels are truly the messengers of God. They are a precious gift that God has given to each and every one of us. —In God's Truth

Catch That Bus

My experience at being an angel began on Boxing Day of 1995. Dad, Mom, and her three sisters, three cousins, and brother-in-law Bill arrived at my house for a turkey dinner. Via the grapevine, I had heard that my uncle Bill had not been well. Consequently, Aunt Josie and he had forgone their usual winter escape to Florida and were available to join the rest of the family for the holiday celebration. However, I was not emotionally prepared for the sight of the skeleton who stepped across my threshold that blustery day after Christmas.

"The man is dying!" a voice screamed inside my head. I tried to control the intensity of my stare as I converted my gaping mouth into a welcoming smile. It did not take long to see that Josie and the others were in a state of denial about Uncle Bill.

Too weak even to sit up at the table, Uncle Bill was helped to the nearest bedroom for a rest. Later, he was roused and cajoled into eating a few spoonfuls of Jell-O. Then, reluctantly, he allowed Aunt Josie to assist him to the living room to witness the opening of presents.

I was the observer. I watched in disbelief as the others flitted around, joking and laughing, seemingly oblivious to this ailing man's fragile state of being. Then guilt set in. Where had I been? Why hadn't I seen this coming? A workaholic, I still did my best to keep in touch weekly with my parents, but months had gone by without contact with other family members.

When it was time to leave, Uncle Bill paused and slowly turned, his eyes locked with mine. "Thank you for having me here today, but I do not really know why I am here," he professed in a clear whisper. "Maybe you just needed to be with family," I promptly replied.

In the hours that followed the din of excitement, amid the chores of cleaning up, I continued to be haunted by the impact of my brief parting exchange with Uncle Bill. There was no doubt that my path and his had crossed for some greater purpose. I prayed for help and guidance.

The next day, I began my daily trips to my aunt and uncle's house, witnessing his coughing spells, the prodding of pills, and the slow spoon-feedings. Cancer is such a silent thief, traveling through the body, robbing each organ of its function and vitality. I watched Uncle Bill's physical form fade away and his mind cloud over those first days of 1996.

The Lions Club donated a hospital bed, which we set up by a sunny window in the living room. A nurse visited regularly to check on the supplies of oxygen and morphine. I learned to juggle my teaching duties so I would have time available in the evenings and on weekends to give Uncle Bill therapeutic touch treatments.

I remember the first time that I came "out of the closet" with my healing abilities, when my dad was present to witness. Aunt Josie was busily talking on the phone, while Dad and I were attempting to visit with my frail uncle.

Gasping for air, Uncle Bill tried to struggle up from the couch to get his wife's attention to call an ambulance. He had become very agitated and could not explain clearly what was happening to him. Dad was urging me to try therapeutic touch to calm Uncle Bill, and I prayed for an angel to guide my hands.

Within moments, Uncle Bill was back on the couch, resting peacefully, to the amazement of the onlookers. I laughed when my dad retold the story later, saying, "If I hadn't seen it myself, I would not have believed it! She actually put him to sleep."

Much to my delight, Uncle Bill began asking for treatments regularly. "Could you do that thing with your hands?" he'd say. Then he would comment on how he thought he must be going crazy because he could feel "it."

I would just laugh and reply, "Well, I must be crazy, because I can feel 'it' too!"

There were times we would talk about heart matters, and Aunt Josie would find out things she had not known about him, such as the time when Uncle Bill's father tried to drown him. My aunt used to say to me, "How did you know to ask him that? He never talked about things like that with me."

I admitted that I did not know what questions I'd ask as I held Uncle Bill's hand, but someone was guiding me and prompting my thoughts about his last wishes. Did he want to be cremated or buried? Who did he want to officiate at his funeral? Who would get the old red truck?

By mid-January, the disease was taking its toll. As Uncle Bill became more depressed, he started expressing how unworthy he felt. He began to wonder, with all his sins, if he would be allowed to go to Heaven.

Again, my angel stepped in as I began to panic over responding to these soul-searching inquiries. Somehow, I found the right words and before I knew it, Uncle Bill was confident and ready to catch what he called "the next available bus."

I hated to leave that night, but a caretaker arrived to stay with Aunt Josie. Reluctantly, I drove home to catch a few winks before that six A.M. alarm would jar me awake and I would scribble a hasty daybook and make myself presentable for another challenging day with a classroom of eager adolescents.

By noon, I was a basket case. I knew something had changed with Uncle Bill. Somehow, a fellow teacher pasted me together and I survived the rest of the day. After school, I wrote up my daybook for the next two days, then rushed over to my uncle's house.

Our communication had dwindled to this: one squeeze of the hand meant "yes" and two squeezes meant "no." I asked Uncle Bill to look for an angel to meet him.

I was sure that the angel who had been speaking through me and helping me for the past three weeks would be there to help him. Two squeezes! Maybe he could see his deceased mother coming to welcome him? No response. I was beginning to sweat. How could I help? My angel had never failed me yet. What was I to do now?

I took a deep breath and asked God for help, and soon I was imagining a beautiful sight. In my mind's eye, I could see Uncle Bill's frail body staggering down a tunnel of light, and just as he was about to stumble and fall, a beautiful angel swooped him up on a soft downy pillow, carrying him the length of the tunnel and into the light.

Suddenly, I was snapped back into my earthly presence by a movement from my comatose uncle. One of his legs was protruding from under the sheet. I chuckled as I realized Uncle Bill wanted to get on that "bus," and that he wanted to go sitting up.

I called to Aunt Josie to get on one side of him while I put my arms under the fluffy pillow supporting Uncle Bill's back. I pulled his heavy weight up until he was in a sitting position.

On January 18, 1999, my precious uncle took his last breath in the arms of his loving wife and niece. I cannot express strongly enough the great honor and momentous occasion that was for me.

My angel stayed with us while we waited for the coroner and ambulance. We had help with the funeral arrangements, and every time we met a roadblock, a better solution resulted. For example, on the day we planned to have the funeral, there were five other burials. There was, so to speak, no room at the inn. So instead of the traditional ceremony, we borrowed chairs, picked up my uncle's ashes and urn, and held his service in the same room from which Uncle Bill had made his transition. I had no prior experience planning for a funeral, nor would I have ever expected to get up and speak at such an emotional time. But speak I did, telling the audience about my angel and our last days with Uncle Bill.

The right books with just the right words fell into my hands. Thanks go to Melody Beattie and Marianne Williamson for their wonderful wisdom and touching messages. (I had not yet discovered *The Messengers* and Nick Bunick's vision of The Great Tomorrow, which would have been so appropriate for the occasion.)

I stayed with my aunt one last night and we talked and talked. I am an only child and she never had any children, so I had not so much lost an uncle as I had gained another mother and dear friend. She thanked me again for being the bridge between her and her husband. I am still amazed at all I did and said. I could tell her only that I had been divinely inspired.

That night while Aunt Josie was getting ready for bed, I placed a gift on her pillow. I had promised Uncle Bill that I would leave her something so that she would know he was always with her. He had not known what to give her, but he was sure that I would find just the right thing when the time was right.

In the bustle of handling the details for the funeral, I remembered my promise and rushed to the nearest gift shop. As I approached the clerk for help, my arm brushed a box by accident, and a shiny golden angel pin fell on the counter by my hand. That angel now rides proudly on Aunt

Josie's collar as a reminder of her husband's love and constant presence. Also, for every birthday, anniversary, and special occasion, an angel of some shape or form arrives at my aunt's house, along with a letter of endearment from her beloved Bill.

It is amazing how one's life can change in such a brief time. How fascinating it is to realize that one meaningful look or that one soft "thank you" could have such profound effects. Angels work in mysterious ways, and I realize now what a sacred privilege it was to care for my Uncle Bill. How thrilled I was to see him overcome his fears and make an effort to step forward into the unknown.

What a blessing for me to be there at that time! I am glad that I accepted the challenge. Maybe sometime you too will grasp the opportunity to be an angel.

Kay Hillman

The Day That Death Transformed Life

My strongest connections to the spiritual/angelic worlds came through my personal experiences of death. I became closer to my soul, to the angels, and to the Kingdom of God. When I feel in my heart what lies ahead at my time of transition, I am filled with love, warmth, and fond memories. My wish is for each individual to find a sense of peace surrounding death.

In 1991, a week after I graduated from college, I had a near-death experience that changed my life forever and made my connection to God and the spiritual world so much more meaningful. Words cannot fully express the feelings I experienced during the time I was with the angels.

Spirit is only a veil away. One minute, I was here experiencing pain and the physical effects of an allergic reaction; and the next, I was in the Light. It was a place of complete, unconditional, and powerful love like I have never felt before. The transition to the spirit world was so easy, just like walking from one room to another. There was no pain, no fear, only love and wings taking me in with compassion. The angels spoke to me through telepathy. The communication is so much deeper there because our vocabulary does not have enough words to communicate all that you receive through the eyes of an angel. The radiant feeling one feels in this beautiful spirit world says more than words could communicate. Life in the spirit world is different than we know here, as there is no time and no barriers.

The angels appeared to me as huge beings of white light, like the intensity of bright sunshine. I did not see any solid forms or faces, but I knew who they were. In this space, I was able to experience the love I have always dreamed of, and that is what it is like there all the time.

Since that experience, I do not fear death anymore. I know what awaits me. I know what beauty, gifts, and warmth lie ahead. This Light and the near-death experience transformed me. Something very powerful happened to me in spirit. I was given a gift and I treasure that experience daily. Life is beautiful and radiant in this light. There is only love and complete acceptance of all. There is no separation or judgments about who you are or what your lifestyle is. If your heart is pure and your intentions are made in love while you are on Earth, that is what counts. You are not cast away, separated, or treated differently based upon your skin color, ethnic background, gender, or the gifts God gave you. What is in your heart counts.

It is an illusion on Earth that we feel that some people are better than others. In the spirit world, we are all the same: beautiful souls radiating the light of who we are. We are all part of God, each one of us. Even those individuals who have done unloving things in their lives are loved. Their angels take special care to be with them upon their death to help them find forgiveness within themselves and to help them understand the consequences of what their behavior was, so they can do better next time.

I used to think God and the angels were somewhere up in the clouds, way far away. I always believed that, based upon what I learned in my Catholic upbringing. Now I know our loved ones are only an angel's wing away. Imagine spirit brushing your cheek. It is that close. Angels really do walk right beside us. Sometimes we just forget to slow down, breathe, and feel their presence. God resides within the heart of each of us.

Another beautiful experience I had took place this past year at the time of my grandma's death. I experienced unconditional love, a powerful healing the angels brought to her to assist her in her transition. I got to feel it strongly again. Her personal angels were with her all day; then an hour before her death, three large angels came to assist her and birth her into the next world. One was at her head and the others were at each side near her feet. These three stayed with her even an hour and a half after her death. I knew she was safe on her journey to spirit.

My family was very comforted as I explained what I felt and saw. It helped them to know the angels were protecting Grandma, guiding and helping her home. Even though they couldn't see anything, they could feel something very special taking place in my grandma's life. The energy of the room felt as though we were in the most beautiful, sacred space. Even at her memorial service and funeral, the angels were by her casket. I could feel their presence, and others could smell a beautiful aroma indicating the angels were close.

After her death, I knew my grandma was not in her body. She was in spirit. I believe the angels surrounded her casket to comfort us as we said our good-byes and remembered her happy days with us. She was there, but not as many would think. She was beside her angels, watching over us.

When I think about my loved ones that have passed to the Light, I know they are in the most beautiful, loving world ever. I miss them and hold them close to my heart and in my memories, and I also smile, knowing how lucky they are to be in the presence of God, the angels, and their loved ones. I still feel sadness that at the time of death, we have to leave behind our loved ones and our physical connections; but at the same time, I know it is part of the divine plan. Our relationship will just be different now. I also know they are so close to us—only a whisper away. They are guiding us in their loving wishes for us. For they hold us in their light and vision.

My time to connect with this unconditional love is during prayer and mediation, sitting in gardens surrounded by flowers and trees, or being by water. These are the times when I am the most relaxed and free to feel their love and presence. I am very grateful for the gift of being able to go to the Light and be surrounded by the angels, with their intense love and guidance. Those memories will always be in my heart. I think passing to the Light is our gift for all the work we do here, however long our experience is on Earth.

Know in your heart that the path to God is the most rewarding path, and it starts today with every meaningful and loving thing we do. Our loved ones who made their transition can help us remember this love when we feel lost or alone. Believe in the power of spirit and it will help you through times of fear, loss, and uncertainty. It works for me when I need it the most.

I want people to be happy and joyous when I die, because I know what it is like to be in spirit. It is magnificent, something to celebrate. I want all loved ones, family, and friends to remember that the bond of love will always remain intact wherever we are and that the light of spirit shines our way to connect us again. That is what our quiet time alone is for—connection to spirit, our loved ones, and to ourselves.

Colleayn T. Klaibourne

The Guardians

Two years ago, we had to move Ruth, my ninety-one-year-old mother-in-law, out of her eleven-room home. She came to live with us. Our home is on a small private lake and it is very quiet. I had always thought Ruth did not like me, but as it turned out, I became responsible for taking care of her. When she arrived, she was in good health, but within two weeks, my husband had me take her to the doctor to determine what was wrong with her. Ruth was a large woman, which made handling her very difficult for me. The doctor gave us the sad news that she had lung cancer and had only one month to live.

The next week, the hospice worker became a part of our lives. We created a bedroom in the living room for my mother-in-law, for it was easier there to tend to her around-the-clock needs. We prayed a lot together, and I tried to find humor in my task. Sometimes it was not easy, but with God's help it worked out.

The Sunday of the fourth week, we were sleeping beside Ruth—my husband on the couch, myself on the floor. At midnight, we heard a loud guttural sound and we woke up immediately, thinking she was dying. Hospice had told us the signs to look for. I told my husband, Paul, that I would sit in the chair beside Ruth until morning. I wrapped a light sheet around myself and decided to pray with my rosary. I am Catholic and Ruth was Methodist, but I figured all prayers go to the same place.

My eyes were closed, and suddenly I saw two huge angels standing guard at the doors. I was astonished. I saw various angels of both genders standing at the foot of her bed. Sitting at the foot of her bed were little angels, cross-legged, looking about three to four years old. At Ruth's side, near her head (in the past week she had been gesturing with her hand, over and over, to a particular spot near her head, saying how beautiful it was) was an old woman angel, and in her arms was a baby angel. I woke my husband, saying, "Paul, look at the angels!" But even after I described them, he could not see them.

Each time I closed my eyes, the angels were watching her. It did not matter whether it was day or night, they were always there. On the following day, Ruth died peacefully as we were saying the Lord's Prayer and touching her. After Paul closed her eyes, he said, "Look and see if the angels are still here." I opened my eyes, but they were gone.

We think the elderly woman spirit was Ruth's mother, who died when Ruth was three years old. The guard angels were her brothers, and the baby was her sister who was a stillborn. I believe I was allowed to be a part of this vision as a gift from God. I believe there are souls and spirits with us at birth and death. With the passing of my mother-in-law, I witnessed that there is no such thing as death.

Sharon Dorland

The Angels and Grandma

These are the true events that took place while I was with Grandma Mandrell during the time leading to her death.

I flew to Lawton, Oklahoma, to be with my grandmother in her last days. She was one hundred years old and had been in good health until recently, when she was diagnosed with cancer. I was obsessed with wanting to be with her when she died, although I cannot tell you why. I loved her a lot, and she asked for me daily, even hourly. I was with her every day beginning on November 9. Grandma knew who I was even though she was in a great deal of pain when she was awake. My sister Maleta and my niece Sheri were her constant companions and caregivers in her last days.

On November 11, everything began to change. We had prayed for Grandma's release from her pain, and this was granted as she slipped into unconsciousness. Aunt Mig, Mom, Maleta, Sheri, Uncle Billy, and I had been staying up with Grandma all night. We did not want her to die alone.

On that night, everyone had gone to bed except Maleta, my brother Bobby, and me. Bobby had spent some time with Grandma, reading and talking to her, saying good-bye. During this same time, I was in the kitchen, and I tried to turn on a television and VCR that I had dusted that day, but they did not work. Suddenly the VCR started flashing 444. (As described in *The Messengers* and *In God's Truth*, 444 means "the power of God's love.") I grabbed Maleta and made her look, and explained that was the sign the angels use. We were both astounded.

Then I went to Grandma's room to be alone with her and to pray for her. I asked the angels to be with Grandma, to comfort her, and fill her room with their presence. My sister joined me, and as I looked up from praying, I was again astounded. I could see a baby of about eight months old sitting at the head of Grandma's bed near her shoulder. The baby was stroking her hair.

I grabbed Maleta's hand and asked if she could see the baby. She could, and she was frightened. I held her hand and told her it was okay, that she need not be afraid. As Maleta calmed down, a small angel appeared in front of me and over Grandma. She was the most beautiful thing I have ever seen in my life! To describe her is impossible, except to say that every detail of her was lit from within in a beautiful bright color. The angel and spirit baby never left Grandma. At first, I had been afraid that they would leave, and then I suddenly knew they were there to stay until Grandma was ready to leave.

Some time had passed. I was now comfortable that the angels were real and were not going to leave Grandma. Maleta was also with me to witness this miracle. I laid my head on Grandma's bed to rest. As I looked up, I saw my breath coming from my mouth as it does on a cold day and it went directly into Grandma's mouth. I felt I was sharing my spirit with her. A gold light encircled both of us, and I could feel someone stroking my hair. I turned to my left and there was a man with a white robe, shoulder-length hair, and beard. His hands were held straight out to his sides. It was his hand that was stroking my hair.

As other members of the family awoke, I brought them in to see the angels. Everyone was at peace when they saw them and understood that death is not frightening, and that the angels come to take you with them so you may be with God.

There were several small children at the house, and oddly, they were filled with peace and understanding about

Grandma's transition. I had gone to the living room to talk to my niece about everything that was unfolding around us. Suddenly, the television turned itself on and started flashing 444. These miracles were no longer shocking us.

In the late afternoon, Grandma began to struggle for her last breaths. She was awake and I began to read the Twenty-third Psalm to her. As I finished the last sentence, I looked into Grandma's eyes and I saw one tear trickle down her cheek. I said, "Go with God, it's okay." Her breathing ceased, Grandma left with the angels as her guides. Her time of death: 4:44 P.M.

Thank you, God, for providing us the understanding.

Sherry Sharabaika

Every one of us was created as a child of God while in the spirit world. Just as a father and mother want to have children, who are created from the life and energy of their parents, God's energy and spirit created us. We are a part of God, each of us having our own individual spirit, which is part of the spirit of God.

—In God's Truth

Harriette

During my mother's illness, I met a kind soul named Harriette, a hospice nurse. She came every morning, doing what most nurses do, and then some. She had that special air about her that let me know in a few minutes of conversation that she was a person who cared.

I had heard from my brothers and sisters how much they and Mom liked her. Harriette is the type of person one is compelled to want to know. She is a tall black woman— nearly six feet tall. Her frame is what you would call large but she is not heavyset. Her loose curls on the top of her head are in contrast to the short cut sides, separated by a fashionable headband, which by itself make her distinctive. To look at her, you might guess her to be in her mid-forties, but she boasts being sixty-three. Her deep brown eyes and dialect add to her formidable presence.

I asked Harriette about a blue pin of a white dove she wore and learned that this was the hospice symbol. Above that, she wore a small gold pin. "That's an angel," she said with pride. "You can't buy one of those. Someone has to give you one." "So you believe in angels, do you?" I asked with a smile. "I sure do," she replied without a moment's hesitation.

"Let me tell you a story," she began. "My daughter was in the hospital with lung cancer. She was thirty-five. There was no cure. She was going to die. I knew it and the doctors knew it. They said there was no cure. She got so bad that at one point, her head swelled to nearly twice its size."

I wanted to ask Harriette what caused the swelling, but I could see in her eyes that she was going someplace else. She was reliving the story as if it had just happened. She was there, seeing things, experiencing them. As she talked, there was no anguish or fear in her voice or on her face. There was only composure, peace, and love, and something else that I can only describe as conviction.

"As I sat by her bed, I prayed to God," Harriette said. "I said, 'Jesus, You've taken my whole family from me. I only have two cousins and my daughter left, and if You want her, You can take her too. She's not only my daughter. She also belongs to You and You can have her back if You want. But Jesus, if You let her stay with me for a while, I promise I'll take good care of her for You.'"

The doctor was sure that Harriette's daughter was going to die. He was about to tell her so, for he happened to be standing in the doorway the day she prayed. He later told Harriette, "I knew she was going to die and I was going to tell you, but when I heard you pray, I couldn't. I just couldn't tell you."

Harriette took a brief moment to tend to my mother, and then continued her story. "My daughter is forty-five now, and she has a lovely daughter who is nine." She said this as if her daughter's recovery should have been obvious to me and needed no further explanation. I smiled knowingly and she smiled back. "I'll get you one of those angel pins," she said, and went back to work.

A few days later, I returned and found the angel pin that Harriette had promised. I held the little treasure in my hand, feeling touched and somewhat special, remembering Harriette's words: "You can't buy one of those. Someone has to give you one."

I never did get a chance to ask Harriette how her daughter was cured or what part angels played in her recovery. I only know that Harriette believes in angels and takes them with her every day, touching other people's lives, one by one.

John Piatek

Good-bye, I Love You

Three years ago, in the fall of 1996, my mother was admitted to a Milwaukee hospital for tests. I had not seen her very much that past summer, so I was shocked to find her extremely thin and frail. She stated with determination that she was going to do whatever it took to beat her illness. We would soon find out just what it would take and how sick she really was.

Her tests and diagnosis led to major surgery. After eleven and a half hours, the surgeon brought us devastating news. Mom had pancreatic cancer, and he had removed portions of five major organs to try to save her life.

Dad and I were allowed to see her in the intensive care unit (ICU) before we left for the night. It was very difficult to control our emotions when we finally saw her after all those agonizing hours of waiting on top of the bad news. Mom was still unconscious from surgery, and she looked as if she had died. I agonized over leaving her like that, so vulnerable and helpless. I asked the angels to watch over her, protect her, and keep her safe while we were gone. It was one of the most difficult days of our lives.

The next morning when we arrived at the ICU, Mom was still sedated but conscious. The first thing she said to me was that she had a dream about angels. I asked her for details, but she would not say anything more. Mom always had a very matter-of-fact personality, and once she made up her mind, she would not change it. She was an extremely strong, independent person and had opinions to match! We had rarely spoken of the softer emotional subjects in our lives, such as angels.

My father and I kept her company and helped care for her for each of the thirty days she was in the hospital. We saw her through several other minor surgeries during that period. Our relationships were forever changed by all the experiences of her illness. From the day my father took her from the hospital back to their home one hundred miles away from me, Mom never ended our telephone conversations without telling me that she loved me.

Mom endured many things over the course of the two and a half years that followed her surgery. She did everything she could to stay with her family and friends for as long as possible. She never completely regained her strength and stamina, but her spirit was as strong as ever. Then on March 29, 1999, I lost the most important woman in my life. Mom had died very suddenly of a heart attack just days after her sixty-seventh birthday. Her illness had worn her down and she left quickly, as she had wanted to when her time came. Her last words to me were, "Good-bye, I love you!"

Throughout the next few days, there were many very trying moments, but in their midst was a bright spot that none of my family will ever forget. At the funeral home, Mom's best friend shared a secret with us that Mom had confided only to her. After her eleven-hour surgery, Mom had regained consciousness in the intensive care unit with no family by her side to comfort her, and she had seen a huge angel in her room watching her.

The angel never spoke a word, but stayed with her for many days until she began to get well again. She continued to see the angel, but he gradually began to fade and was eventually gone. She never spoke a word about her angelic encounter to anyone except her friend. A few months prior to Mom's death, my husband and I had been taking an angel awareness class. I hesitantly mentioned the class and some other metaphysical interests of ours to Mom on the phone one day. I remember her saying, "I don't know about that other stuff, but I think the angel class might be a good idea!"

Yes, Mom, you knew. I hope you know. I love you too.

Diane Koser

A Heavenly Experience

She was "Grandma Ruthie" to most of us who knew her well. She was a fun-loving, happy person who was loved by all. She had reached the age of ninety-five, and due to a back injury, was confined to a nursing home. Her mind was still very clear and her soul and personality were shining as brightly as ever. She spent her days making the best of an unfortunate situation by helping anyone she could, in any way she could. This was usually accomplished by being a good listener and offering loving and spiritual advice to those who wished to talk.

Grandma Ruthie had been a registered nurse for many years and had worked most of them in the obstetrics ward of her local hospital. She helped bring new little lives into the world and gave good counsel to the new mothers. She was well loved there. Grandma Ruthie was a spiritual person if there ever was one. She was a reader of esoteric material and a student of philosophy and life in general. Many of us who were close to her realized she was an "old soul" who had been around many times and learned much. She radiated comfort, goodness, and God's grace.

Her goal now was to prepare herself for the journey into the next realm. She said she was ready to leave anytime. During the interim before her passing, she and I had some great discussions together. We talked of many things and pondered and wondered. During these talks, she told me that she wanted to share a strange experience that she had been having since she had moved to the rest home. It is a fascinating and beautiful story.

Her first remark before she started her narration was, "I don't expect anyone to really believe this, and I myself know that it sounds impossible, but it is true and has happened four or five times to me. It is not the product of senility or delusions." I wasn't sure where she was taking me this time, but I listened with my mind open wide. Her delivery was straightforward and without hesitation. As I listened, I felt strongly that Grandma Ruthie had experienced all that she was relating.

Three or four times a week, she was awakened by "something" in the early morning hours. She could see two figures standing at the foot of her bed who were dressed in white with a golden light around them. They introduced themselves as a brother-and-sister team. Their names were Sylvia and Edwin, they told her, and they made the nightly rounds of many hospitals and nursing homes to comfort, care for, and console any patient in need.

Grandma Ruthie sensed a deep feeling of peace and love as she looked and listened. These two "helpers" produced a cover of soft gossamer, a shining, gauzelike material, with which they wrapped any person who was lonely, cold, or unhappy. This material had no weight but was extremely warm and comforting. Within minutes, the patient was again warm, dry, relaxed, and sound asleep. After waving good-bye with a smile and a "God bless," Sylvia and Edwin would go up four small steps and disappear.

I had to ask, what happened to the sheer gossamer coverlet and didn't the attendants and nurses notice it when they arrived in the morning? Grandma Ruthie's answer was, "As morning comes and dawn breaks, the covers seem to disintegrate and are gone when they are no longer needed. Besides, they wouldn't be noticed by anybody who didn't believe in these things and wouldn't be looking for them."

Grandma Ruthie seemed thrilled about these occurrences, so it made me happy that she shared her story with me about these two heavenly beings. There is no doubt in my mind that it is all true. It wasn't many weeks after our talk that she made her transition. I feel she is in her right place and maybe even working now with Sylvia and Edwin. Who knows?

Both of us knew that experiences such as these prove the existence of angels and life after death, and that we are all entering a new dimension where we will have a new beginning after completing our time here on Earth.

In 1992, six years after the death of Grandma Ruthie, our granddaughter Melinda and her husband lost their seven-month-old baby girl, Kailyn. She was born with a defective heart and only one kidney.

She had been in the hospital several weeks. When our granddaughter was told of the baby's death, she left the room and went out into the hall. It was a long, empty corridor. As she walked slowly towards the far end, she saw a nurse coming toward her, an older woman who was walking slowly. As they got closer to each other, Melinda recognized the nurse. It was her great-great-grandmother, Grandma Ruthie, who had died in 1986. Not a word was spoken, nor was there a sound in the empty hall. Melinda was shaken and overwhelmed, but she knew without any doubt who was there with her. The "nurse" smiled warmly at her and looked deep into her eyes as they passed each other. When Melinda turned around to look at her again, she had disappeared.

For both young parents, it eased some of the pain in their hearts. They were able to go on because they realized that little Kailyn was in God's loving care alongside her great-great-grandmother.

Ruth Ann Poindexter

The Witness

My father was in his ninety-third year and he was looking forward to being ninety-four. But a stroke gradually put him in his bed, and continuing small strokes dimmed his light considerably.

Hospice guided both of us through the rough waters until I was told that the time of his death was very near and that there were signs I should expect to precede it.

The next morning, I placed two candles at the foot of my father's bed, on his television set so he could see them. The next time I entered his room, both the candles were out. But there were no windows open and there was no draft to extinguish them. I lit both candles again. They burned brightly and filled his room with a quiet peace, but within an hour, the candles were out again. I was then sure that my father's light would also soon be extinguished.

The next morning, I looked into his room and I was astounded, taken aback. There at the foot of his bed stood two angels. They nearly touched the ceiling. They wore flowing white robes and had long hair, with their wings folded against their backs. They faced my father and I could not see him in his bed. I was allowed the incredible vision just for an instant. This was an extraordinary gift to me that was manifested by universal love and peace.

When I went to his bedside, he had already made the transition. Now my father's suffering was over and he was in the company of his angels and God. Thank you, God, for allowing me to be a witness.

M. O'Leary

Our minds are the gatekeepers of our hearts and souls. Millions of people throughout the world have now opened their gates and are allowing information to come into their hearts and souls that otherwise they would not receive. —In God's Truth

Our Journeys

All of us are on the same journey through life. But let us travel back to a time when mankind did not have written words and had few means of communication, when even speech was very limited—a time we would describe as a primitive world.

Our primitive ancestors witnessed a child growing into an adult. They witnessed the bodies and skills and minds of the adults eventually deteriorating. They witnessed "life" leaving the bodies of the ones they knew as their parents, their companions, and their loved ones. They had no religious leaders to preach to them of a Heaven or a Hell. The Bible had not yet been written, so they had no exposure to the concept of a creator, or to the scientists and academic proponents of evolution.

But they understood the personality of nature. They

saw night turn into day, and then again into night. They experienced the warmth of summer, which was eventually replaced by the chill of winter, then again, the start of spring and warm weather until fall and coldness returned, year after year.

They saw the birth of leaves on the trees, the deterioration of the leaves falling to the ground in the autumn, the bareness of the branches in winter, only to be reborn again with beautiful new green buds in the spring. Through their own simple logic, they understood the cycle of life and the system that nature was manifesting in their daily lives. It was no wonder that in the absence of religious teachings, and in the absence of scientists and academics, our ancestors who lived in these primitive societies realized that death was not a finality, was not an ending of life, but rather, the recycling of a life. In actuality, our primitive relatives of many thousands of years ago were the first New Age believers.

Mankind eventually became more sophisticated and educated. The less intellectual understandings of the natural belief systems of those societies were eventually replaced. New belief systems came to be formed, and there were many, many different concepts, depending on the culture, the attitudes, and the teaching of those individuals who were held as authorities.

In the Mideast, people viewed death as a separation of the body and spirit of the deceased. They believed the spirit ascended to another location and would exist at that place throughout eternity. Other societies believed in the transmigration of the soul, which today we refer to as reincarnation. Still others believed in the annihilation and termination of the soul at the time of death.

But immortality was an absolute belief in some of the oldest writings throughout the world. The Tasmanian, Samoan, and Asian societies believe that a soul surely survives after death. In the Egyptian Book of the Dead, written approximately 3,500 years before the death of Jesus, it is written that the human soul is eternal and exists forever.

One of the greatest minds in Greek philosophy had

another concept. Pythagoras, who was born 500 years before the birth of Christianity, thought that the soul continues to come back into human life form over and over again, until it reaches perfection, and then it is reunited with God. In other words, birth is preceded by death, and death is the advent of the future birth of the soul into a newborn child.

I embrace this belief system of Pythagoras, which he had 2,500 years ago. I believe life is a revolving door into the spiritual world; or if you prefer, the spiritual world is a revolving door into the mortal world. As we enter the world, regardless of what period in history or time it is, we enter through our mother's womb into a huge room called life. As we make our way through this room, we encounter many incredible challenges. We must learn to conquer hunger, to survive pestilence and disease, to avoid being a casualty of war, or perhaps a victim of mankind's cruelty against his fellow man.

When we finally succeed in meeting and surviving all of these challenges, we then come to that golden door at the opposite side of the room, the door that takes us across the threshold into the spiritual world—the door that is called death.

Why is it necessary for those who were our teachers, our poets, our scientific scholars, and yes, even in some cases, our religious leaders, to portray that doorway as filled with fear, with uncertainty, with doubt, with sadness, with threats of punishment, or with the possible termination of our minds and existence? Some even preach of a punishing God who may be displeased with us because we did not live our lives consistent with the guidelines of our religious leaders.

That is the death that has died and should never have lived. I do not believe in that kind of death, the kind riddled with fear and uncertainty. I know that the spirit of God resides in every one of us, that we are all God's children, that we are immortal and eternal because of the gift God has given to each of us.

Is it not time again for us to embrace the understanding that was embodied by even our most primitive ancestors before their beliefs were tainted by those who would have us believe otherwise? Can we not change the concept of death, and let us have the word "death" die? Let us instead adopt the truth that the culmination of our physical body creates a transition of our spirit and soul into the spiritual world. In so doing, not only do we manifest the truth of the system that God created, but we can also substitute for the word "death" the term "spiritual transition." For truly, then, death will have died, as we allow our spirits to live on as they will.

Nick Bunick

Part Three

Sights, Smells, and Sounds

There are many ways for our loved ones to come to us, to affirm that they are still living in spirit, and that there is no such thing as death, but only a transition of our mortal body into a pure spiritual form when it no longer continues to function.

My brother, who was four years older than I, died when he was in his fifties. I have often said sarcastically that he gave his life to the tobacco companies, for he was a chain smoker. This addictive habit eventually cost him his life. I always associated his leaving us as a result of this tobacco addiction.

At two different times in the last eighteen months, there was a tremendously strong odor of cigarette smoke around me twenty-four hours a day, in spite of the fact there are no smokers in my family or office. Even though I had no contact at all with cigarette smoke, the smell of smoke would stay with me for entire days, usually several days at a time.

The first time it happened, I called a dear friend of mine who was a nationally recognized clairvoyant. She told me a member of my family who had passed over was visiting with me and letting me know that he was fine by using the cigarette smell as a means to identify his presence. After she told me this, I then acknowledged my brother's presence and asked him for forgiveness for anything I had done in my relationship with him that required forgiveness. I also forgave him for anything he felt he may have done to cause me anguish. We had a good relationship, and I do not know if forgiveness was an issue in it, but I wanted him to know that I loved him and acknowledged him. Shortly after these acknowledgments, the cigarette smell disappeared and I knew his spirit was no longer around me.

In this next series, you will find stories about unique signs associated with deceased loved ones. These signs range from recognizing aromas of a loved one who is deceased to chimes or other signs that the storyteller shares with us.

These heartwarming accounts will take you in many different directions, but the most important direction is hearing from the writers that it brought them great joy and comfort, for they knew that their loved ones were providing them a sign that they were okay and happy. These signs let them know that there is no such thing as death, but only a transition into the spirit world.

Nick Bunick

Don't Close the Door

Dearest Mama,

Mama. I always wanted to say it out loud but it never fit somehow. Sometimes you were Mother, sometimes Mom. But deep in my heart, where my little child-self still dwells, you are Mama. I am going to address you as Mother in this letter just like I always did, but please hear the echo of my heart beat out to you, Mama.

Those last forty days when you were in the hospital were so difficult for us who loved you so much and couldn't imagine life without you. Actually, for the first twenty or so of those days, we didn't know that you were going to die. We never spoke of that possibility, did we? Each day, as we came to visit you, we thought that maybe this would be the day you recovered, that we would walk in the room and you would be the mother (and grandmother) we had always known, not the gradually diminishing shell our eyes so sadly saw lying in the hospital bed.

I kept a journal, Mother, during your death process. I think you knew this. I carried it with me when I visited you, sometimes writing down my thoughts and the events of the day while you rested or as the nurses tended to your needs. You never asked about the journal or what I was writing.

It was only later, some months after you died,

that I appreciated the enormity of the gifts you gave me those last forty days you remained on Earth before you went home. It was only when I read, in my own handwriting, the chronology of our conversations, the veiled messages you related from higher dimensions, your openness in sharing with me the stages of your death process, that I realized you gave me a gift beyond measure.

There are some things I need to tell you, Mother, about those last several years before you died. It was really hard for me, even though I was nearing my middle years, to make the break from you in relation to my spiritual pursuits. It was difficult to know that you didn't approve of my seeking spirituality outside the traditional teachings of the Church. But I had to, Mother. I knew that too often ministers and priests teach the limitations of their own minds and ascribe those limitations to God.

It must have been hard for you sometimes to have a daughter like me. Ever since I was a little girl, I had to ask the why and how questions endlessly. Growing up, I learned to keep those questions to myself, but I didn't stop wondering. As adamant as you were about your fundamental religious beliefs, I was equally determined to find my own path. I know it was frightening to you that your daughter studied ancient wisdom teachings, dream symbology, Eastern philosophies; that she practiced meditation and talked about the higher meanings of Jesus' teachings. I know you simply wanted to protect me and you were afraid I was going to be hurt by some strange book or someone who would lead me astray.

I am a mother too, and I know how deep our mothering instincts are. I'm sorry I challenged you so severely that day, soon after my divorce, when you referred to me as your child and I so fiercely declared that I was not your child, that I was your adult daughter, and I banged my arm on your table for emphasis. My children were much younger then, so I didn't know that there is a place so special in a mother's heart that even when her children become grown-up, become adult men and women to us, we still see and cherish the child in them.

I didn't know the magnitude of this truth until I discovered and honored my own child-self not so long ago. But that is another story.

As I sit here writing this letter to you, Mother, I know that our impasse at that time was due to the ongoing lessons that each of us struggled with. Yours was communication and mine was injustice. It's so clear now. You were not able to convey to me that you could see and love both the adult and the child in me. I didn't think it was fair that, after all the challenges I had dealt with in my life, my years of studying and accomplishing, you still thought I was only a child. I felt I needed your approval and you felt that I should know that I was your child and you were the parent and that was that. Now I understand the fullness of your love.

I do thank you, Mother, for acknowledging an important aspect of our mother/daughter relationship, even though I wasn't ready to accept it at the time. It took time for me to come full circle. I was so bent on finding my own identity separate from you. I did find what I was looking for, and in the process, I discovered our oneness.

Now I see the order, as well as the beauty, in my spiritual awakenings during those last years of your Earth life. A part of me would have loved to tell you about them, but I felt the gulf between our belief systems too great to bridge at the time. How I wished I could have shared with you the great earth-shattering experience I had early one morning, just months before you got sick. It was an experience that changed every cell of my body and the blood that coursed through my veins.

I had awakened at four-thirty that morning and felt very strongly guided to stay awake. I sat at your kitchen table, only a few yards from your bedroom door, candlelight softly illuminating the room, alone with my thoughts.

That morning, the heavens split open and I learned that this Earth-life is a mere and dark shadow. I knew what the Apostle Paul meant when he said, "For now we see through a glass darkly; but then face-to face."

Something happened to me that morning, Mother. I went "Home." But it wasn't time to stay. Not yet. That morning I learned about the Light. That morning I learned about love.

So when you began sharing your experiences with me as you prepared to go Home, I had to find that delicate balance between my happiness for you and my selfish sorrow of giving you up in this physical world. When the thought of your death crept in, I pushed it away, but eventually I could evade it no longer.

Now I know that if I had not had my awakening, I would not have known how to react to your experiences. I may have thought you were hallucinating.

The moment I walked into your room on the eighteenth day of your hospitalization, I knew something was wrong. You were sitting up in bed with a soft drink cup on the tray in front of you. I bent over to kiss you and you whispered, "Be careful."

To my usual questions of how your day had been and if the doctor had been in, you answered in little frightened whispers or slight nods. Something wonderful had begun, but religion had not prepared you for the process.

Your eyes were filled with fear and anxiety as you searched my face and the far corners of the room. I sat next to you a long while, my love and strength flowing into you as I held your hand. Finally, when you weren't shaking so badly, you reached for a card on the bedside table and traced a pitiful plea with your index finger: "Help." Then you turned the card over.

I took your hand again and softly queried, "Help, Mother?" You motioned for me not to speak aloud, and again searched the room with your eyes. Haltingly, you began telling me something of what you had experienced. You said, "It's all done with mirrors and they can see everything. I'm not sure what it means yet, but it is about a school and the hospital is part of it."

My heart was pounding as I stroked your hand and assured you that no one would hurt you. I stayed with you, easing you back onto the pillows, until I felt fairly sure you were calm and felt safer. Then I drove to Phyllis's house to tell her of this new development. We agreed that we should return to the hospital to be with you until we were sure you were no longer frightened.

When we entered your room, you were not sleeping, and we saw that you were still very frightened. So we sat, your two daughters, one on each side of your bed, holding your hands in silence. Loving you. Soon it was obvious that you were entering another realm of consciousness, speaking in phrases, some of which we could understand and others we could not quite make out. It seemed that you were talking to and answering beings we could not see.

Then the anxiety came back and you told us about the fire and pleadingly asked us if anyone had called for the fire trucks. You said the fire was all around your head and you were so afraid. I bent low to you, feeling as though I were the mother, you my child, and asked if you would like to pray, and you said yes. Together, the three of us recited the Lord's Prayer as never before, and then I led us through the Twenty-third Psalm. You begged, "Jesus, have mercy," over and over until your acceptance of love extinguished the flames of your belief in Hell.

Leaning down to you again, I told you about the Light. "Mother, one day soon you will see a great and beautiful Light. Don't be afraid, Mother. Go into the glory of God."

"A Light?" you asked.

"Oh yes, Mother, a beautiful Light," I told you with certainty. You said you would remember, and then I reminded you of the dream you had several days earlier of David, your beautiful son in Heaven. You laughed as you remembered the dream and then you fell asleep peacefully.

I am so grateful I had the opportunity the next day to tell you that I was glad you were the one who was my mother and that we will always be a part of one another in spirit and through the cycles of generations of your offspring.

That night and other nights, we saw you having lively conversations with beings in higher realms. At one point, you told us you were thinking about seeing Dad and David, and I smelled roses. Phyllis walked into the room just then and said, "I smell roses." You fell asleep for a while and then, as we watched in wonder, you lifted your hand, smiled radiantly, and gently waved three or four times to someone we couldn't see. You clearly said, "Come on in." Then, after a few moments of quiet, you slowly raised your hand, and finding the top of your head, almost in slow motion, you patted yourself three times in a very satisfied manner. I had the distinct feeling that you had passed an important test and that you had graduated. Oh, Mother, both my sister and I are forever blessed to have witnessed on this side of the veil, in the company of your special angels and teachers, your graduation ceremony.

You asked the nurses to bathe and dress you in your prettiest new gown and we stayed with you until you fell asleep. As we were leaving, I looked back at you, and I could swear that I saw a halo of light above your head.

After that, I clearly saw you withdrawing more and more from Earth-life. One day you told me, "The plans have changed. They are helping someone else first. I don't know the name." So we waited, all of us who loved you so much, the days and nights taking their toll on our energy. The doctors and nurses really could not tell us much. In fact, they tried their best to avoid direct answers.

But in the waiting and the observing, we became aware of a divine timing to the events of each day. Indeed, there were selected moments when we felt that everything was being choreographed from above.

One evening, tired and sad, I sat on a bench outside the hospital gazing at the autumn sunset. For a long time, I watched clouds moving into and through patterns of light and streaks of blended color, feeling suspended in space and time. Calmed and lifted by the beauty of the western sky, I saw groups of clouds coming together from all directions, then remaining fixed as they met. I envisioned that out of the center of the clouds and light, Christ stepped forward, a huge figure in the sky. His arms were outstretched to me and I entered His love, closed my eyes, and felt Him in the center of my being.

On the last day of your life, Mother, I somehow knew it was the last day. You were alert and free from pain. From time to time, I watched you speak soundlessly to beings above you. I saw you strain upward to them several times, and once I saw your lips move with the silent words, "I love you." Two or three times, I felt cool air pass by me as I sat beside you, holding your hand for hours, trying not to intrude as you prepared to cross over.

Becoming aware of hammering noises out in the hall, I told you they were installing new carpet and that I would shut the door. Your hand quickly guided me back down in the chair. You focused your eyes squarely into mine and said, "No. Don't shut any doors. Don't close the door."

Those were the last words you spoke to me. I knew you were not speaking just about the hospital door. Your spirit spoke to my spirit, and I heard your approval of my spiritual path as you told me during your energy transfer that I must keep all doors open— the doors of my heart, my mind, and my soul—on my journey. And you knew that I had heard you.

Moments after your last gentle breath, I looked down at the body you had used while you attended this school of life, the body you no longer needed, for you had matriculated to another dimension of life. I looked at the body and it was empty. What a realization to understand that your body was not really you.

Coming from that realization, I heard my own words ringing in my ears, "My God! Mother." For the Light you had entered still faintly glowed around your form on the bed, although you had already stepped across the threshold, through the open door, and gone Home.

I've pondered your messages many times over the years, Mother. It's all done with mirrors, Mother? It's about a school and they know everything? The fire around your head. Roses. You graduated. Conversations with beings above you. "I love you." "No. Don't shut any doors. Don't close the door." These messages blessed me as you have blessed me.

Sometimes I look in the mirror and it almost scares me. I see you. Sometimes I look at one of your grandchildren or my sister and brothers, and I see you. But not just the physical appearances. No, it is more than that. I see your spirit. Little by little, Mother, my capacity to see has expanded, because now I can see beyond our family. I can see now, in the eyes of my fellow Earth travelers, the spirit of love that I first saw on Earth: you. Mama.

Light and Love,

Mary Lou

Mary Lou Homer

If you placed a hundred people in a room, all of whom truly understood their relationship with God and were in harmony with that part of God that is inside of them, their own immortal spirit and soul, and you asked them, "Are you happy?"—they would all say yes. For it is being in harmony with your own spirit and soul that is part of God that brings you true happiness.

—In God's Truth

Don't Worry, Be Happy

On December 22, 1988, my father decided to finally let go of his battle with cancer, the monster he had feared all his life. I was a twenty-two-year-old university student then, and before the last six months of his life, I would have never believed anyone who told me my dad, my hero, would be the first one in the family to leave.

Everyone dutifully embarked on the journey with him.

My mother was the first to ask him to leave his house and to stay with her at her home. They had been amicably separated since I was seven. She prided herself in being his strength through this very difficult and emotional road they would be traveling together. He still had some lessons to learn and a few people to make amends with. He was always strong about finalizing things, and I believe he felt it was his responsibility to show a good example about all of this to his family, to the ones he had been so proud of, and had so loved.

He had the time to have special talks with all of us and even put in writing a few loving words of wisdom for us. He encouraged us and told us to be strong and to focus on the big picture, to love each other, to be good examples, and above all to remember that God had the final word and that He would never let us down.

We all thought that we would be spending Christmas at the hospital with him that year, but I don't think he wanted that. The last night, as I walked into his hospital room, he had the most reassured look in his eyes, and his first words to me were, "You're an angel!" Of course, my tears kept falling all night as I was wiping his forehead or blinking his eyes for him. I watched as each breath became more and more difficult. I was holding his hand, his arm, and some-times his entire body. He was so frail. I was aware that he still wouldn't let go before he knew for sure that at least one of my brothers would arrive to take his place as the pillar of the family. This meant to take care of the family business, to take charge of the family finances, and to make sure that everyone was okay.

In my heart, I knew that it wasn't about me, my mother, or my brothers anymore. It was his passing, and as he had said before, we all embarked upon this journey together six months before to grow spiritually. I knew that I would be the one to close his eyes. I was waiting to do that one last thing for him.

Did he know that act alone would make me strong? Did he know that this journey would motivate me to read every-thing I could get my hands on regarding death after he had passed? Did he know that I would learn to let him go and wish him well? Did he know that I believed him when he said he would keep a close eye on us after his death?

Oftentimes, before his transition, he would let us know

that he was between worlds. It was beautiful. As he took his last breath, I told my father, "Go in peace, Daddy. I will always love you."

I can still feel him around me today, sometimes making me laugh. For example, one hour after his passing, the very first words of a song that I heard while we were driving from the hospital were, "Don't worry. Be happy." He had such a sense of humor. I know he appreciates it when I talk out loud to him, even when the people around me probably think I am crazy. I'm just letting him know that I got it. I now know that we are only here for a short time, but are together forever.

Ella Godin Lacroix

Baby Marc's Life Story

Our family entered 1960 in not the best financial condition. My husband Paul was laid off work for the winter. He was a carpenter by trade, and there was no work available at that time. He was collecting unemployment, but that was only about $200 a month and our rent was almost half of that at $75. Thank heavens, that winter the government gave each member of the family of a person on unemployment a case of canned meat. We got sixty cans, which helped with the grocery bill.

I was in the ninth month of my fourth pregnancy. My twenty-second birthday was at the end of January, and my baby was due around the twenty-fifth. I wasn't looking forward to this child as I was worried about how we were going to feed everyone. After having three children already, I had few baby clothes left. An aunt who lived on a farm gave me some nighties made out of flour sacks. I felt bad that I would have to use these, because I liked flannelette for babies. It was soft and cuddly like they are. I would never have thought of abortion, because I love little babies. They need you so much. I remember how important I felt after I had my first child at seventeen, as if I had done something that no one else could have. It is true, since no one else can have the exact same child as you can.

The evening of January 22, my husband drove me to the hospital in his old truck after we dropped the other three little ones at my mom's. My pains were only a few minutes apart, so they prepped me right away after I was admitted. Then my water broke and I got scared. One of my older sisters' water broke with her first baby and she was in labor for two days before he was born. Meanwhile, my pains stopped altogether and nothing was happening. All was quiet as I lay there in the dark.

I started thinking of the child inside of me. How scared he must be too. I started to talk to him. "Don't be scared little one. It will be all right. It is the only way you can get out of there. Give it another try. I'll be waiting to hold you as soon as you enter this world. You have a big brother who is four, and two big sisters, two and a half and twenty months old, waiting for you. You can do it. Don't be scared." I fell asleep, trusting God that everything would go well.

Early in the morning, I woke because the pains had started up again with full force. In no time at all, I had a new little son. He was beautiful and perfect, and there had been no trouble at all with the delivery.

When I took him home, I had to put him in the armchair in front of the oil burner in the living room. The house we lived in had only three rooms, and the little bedroom already had a double bed for us, a bunk bed for the two older children, and a crib for the baby girl. There was no room for another crib in the room, and we couldn't afford another crib anyway.

He was such a good baby, who hardly ever cried. I phoned one of my sisters to tell her what a beautiful baby he was, and said, "Sal, he is such a good baby, like a little angel. He's too good for this world." I would regret those words later.

One month and four days later I woke up about six A.M. because the baby hadn't cried during the night. His little hands were out of the blanket and cold. I tucked in his hands and took him to bed with us. He seemed to have a sniffle. About an hour later, a neighbor came to borrow the blowtorch to thaw out his water pipes. As our house was only three rooms with one door, you would come into the kitchen, where we had a coal and wood range for cooking, then into the living room, where there was an oil-burning heater, and then into the bedroom, where there was no heat. Our house had cold water coming into a sink in the kitchen, but when the temperature outside went to around minus thirty degrees Fahrenheit, my husband would have to go down into the little six-by-six-foot dirt cellar under the kitchen floor and thaw out the pipe with a blowtorch, just as our neighbor had to do on this morning.

I got up and answered the door and called my husband. He got out of bed and went to the door, but I had a feeling to go check on the baby. He was cold and not breathing. I screamed to my husband and ran out with the baby in my arms. There was no 911 to call in those days, so I phoned our doctor. He said he would send an ambulance. I tried to give the baby artificial respiration, but I didn't know how to do it and realized I hadn't squeezed his nose closed. The ambulance took him away, and my husband jumped in his truck and followed.

Baby Marc was dead on arrival at the hospital. The doctor explained that a baby's lungs are only the size of a quarter and sometimes babies die even in between nurses' rounds in the hospital, and there was nothing they could do. Today they call it SIDS, Sudden Infant Death Syndrome, but I don't think they had a name for it back then.

Although I didn't understand God's reason for taking the little fellow so young, I accepted his death because I was brought up to believe that God had a reason for everything.

After the funeral, the florist arrived at our house with a chrysanthemum plant, which I then placed on the table in the living room. An aunt had also sent some little presents for the children, presents she had forgotten to send at Christmas. I placed these beside the plant. When I gave the children these gifts, our four-year-old announced to his little sisters that these gifts were from Baby Marc's tree. I guess in his mind he was getting Christmas mixed up with these gifts that were under Baby Marc's plant. We had explained to the children that the baby had gone to Heaven, but he was still part of our family and still called Baby Marc.

Twenty-nine years later, I had an opportunity to have a reading by a trance medium. I was interested in this kind of stuff, but my husband told me I was crazy, so I never shared anything of this sort with him. I sent questions to the medium, who would go into a trance, and his wife would ask the questions on my behalf. You had to mention the address of each person you inquired about so the medium could locate them, and you had to also include their date of birth.

It was a one-hour reading, and the last question I had asked was why each of our children—and I listed each by name and date of birth, including Baby Marc—had chosen us for parents. They had to give a short answer because there was only a minute or two left of my allotted hour. The answer was something to this effect: "Each of these children thought you offered them the opportunity to learn the lessons they needed to learn in this life, even the one that only needed the birthing experience."

I was so elated to hear this. It explained everything to me about Baby Marc's unusual delivery, his perfect, angelic look, and why he was with us such a short time. I was so happy that he chose me for that birthing experience. I cried. I felt so wonderful to have aided him in this spiritual experience, although I hadn't thought of it as a spiritual experience at the time. Now, however, I can see how each birth is a spiritual experience, a miracle.

Everything fit so perfectly, like all God's lessons, once we can see with hindsight the whole picture. What better time for this child to choose to come into this world and leave so quickly than when the parents were experiencing hard times and didn't know how they were going to feed this new baby when they had three other children under five years old. So the words I said to my sister that I had regretted for years were the truth: he was a little angel; he was too good for this world.

About five years after this trance medium reading, I was participating in a therapy workshop to learn who I was and what made me tick. I have been involved in these group experiences for seventeen years and have had some profound revelations during meditation and relaxation exercises. Usually afterwards when I went home at night, I would have dreams or experiences related to what we were working on in the workshop. This time I woke up at five A.M. and wrote some poetry, which I enjoy doing. I was so grateful for my children, I wrote a poem about each one and took these to the workshop the next morning, to share with the group. I would like to share with you the one I wrote about Baby Marc:

Baby Marc,
my little one,
You were so afraid to come
into this world;
So you took your time.
I was scared too.
I had never waited so long
for a baby to be born.
But we made it,
you and I.
I didn't realize the value
of the treasure
as I held you in my arms.
But just holding you
erased my resentment at your timing.

You were really
too good for this world.
Such a fine soul,
so delicate,
and so brave!
We had such a short time
together, you and I.

But it was quality time;
it had to be
to last my lifetime.
I'm looking forward
to meeting you again
when my work here is done.
In my memory you remain
my little one
whom I love.

June 16, 1984
Love, Mom

I wrote six poems that morning. Christmas 1995, the year before I lost my job due to downsizing, we were strapped at Christmas and I didn't know how I was going to get presents for all the children and grandchildren, so I typed up each of these poems, framed them, and gave them to my children for gifts. Thank you, dear Lord, for the blessings you have bestowed upon me.

Alice M. A. Lalonde

Control what goes into your mind. Happy thoughts produce happiness. Sad thoughts produce sadness. An onion seed produces an onion. Love is the greatest elixir of all. It cleanses our soul, erases negative feelings, makes us tolerant, patient, caring, interesting, enthusiastic.

—In God's Truth

Christmas Spirit

My sister and best friend, Patricia Lynn Cosgrove, was horseback riding when she was hit by a car and killed. The accident was on August 24, our mother's birthday. Patty was thirteen, I was fourteen, so we were close in age and in heart; but as is true with most siblings, we also had our arguments.

That dark day started out as a beautiful, carefree summer Saturday in what had been a fun summer of discovery as we blossomed into our teens. However, on that day, as we readied ourselves to go riding, a power play erupted over a blouse we both wanted to wear. The deciding factor was that Patty had it on first, so she won the battle. I was so angry about not getting my way, I decided not to go with her and the other riders.

I will never forget the last time I saw my sister, the image of her walking away, thick chestnut ponytail swinging back and forth, wearing that blouse. That image was burned into the core of my soul by my searing remarks. The last words my beloved little sister heard from me as she walked away were, "I hope you have a terrible day." She did. She died two hours later.

Patty's loving spirit was too strong and she cared too much to let that ugliness be our last interaction. Our spiritual bond enabled us to overcome the illusion of separation. She probably attempted many times to make her presence known to me after she died, but it took seven years for her to get my attention.

Our family was celebrating Christmas at our mountain cabin. All day long, I had the sensation of someone missing. When we sat down for dinner, I said, "We have to wait for . . ." But I couldn't say and didn't know who we might be waiting for, because everyone was present. The same feeling came over me when we started to open the gifts. I felt we had to wait for one more person to take a warm, comfortable seat around the fireplace. I didn't know that I was sensing the spirit of someone I couldn't see.

Finally, we all went for an early evening walk in the newly fallen snow. I was bringing up the rear. I felt someone's energy behind me and again thought we had to wait. When I turned around and saw no one there, I said to myself, "Okay Patty, if you are here, I want you to make the snow fall from a tree like an avalanche."

I continued to walk with my family, and when I passed under a big tree, I felt the branches bend toward me as a load of snow knocked me down! Only me—and in the exact way I had pictured in my mind when I made the request.

My father ran back to me in fear that I had been hurt. I was exhilarated, laughing with joy, transfixed for a moment in the realm of pure love and bright light as our spirits embraced. I was in touch with and touched by an angel, my sister. After this spectacular manifestation, Patty continued to communicate with me. I have many other stories about her communication with me, as well as with my precious father, who has now joined her on the Other Side.

Although I have been doing healing work for many years, I became aware that I am a spiritual medium only a year ago. As I wrote this story, it dawned on me that my gift as a medium is most likely the result of that first experience so long ago. It has taken me almost three decades to realize that a portal between our physical and spiritual worlds opened up for me that Christmas Day.

Thank you, Patty.

Kathlyn Stabile

You Will Always Be My Baby

We were blessed to have Dad with us an additional six years after he suffered a ruptured aneurysm, which the doctors said he should not have survived. I thanked God for sparing him a sudden death, which gave me the extra time I needed to let him know how much I loved him and how grateful I was to have such a strong role model. He was always my source of strength and inspiration. Even though I have two brothers, I was his only little girl. This is a position in the family that I always treasured.

As Dad's health deteriorated, I prayed that when it was his time, God would take him quickly so that he would not have to suffer for an extended period of time in a hospital or nursing home. My prayers were answered early one morning, when my mother phoned to inform me that Dad had passed away peacefully in his sleep only minutes before.

As I drove to be by mother's side, I grieved for my loss, but especially for that of my mother. I had complete faith that Dad was at peace and in a much better place. The days, weeks, and months that followed were taken up with funeral arrangements, with the family coming in from out of town and helping my mother adjust to her life without Dad. They had been so close for more than fifty years. My heart ached for my mother, who was trying her best to be strong for all of us. I missed Dad terribly, but I didn't take any personal time to adjust to my life without him.

We live in Phoenix, Arizona, so Mom and I thought it would be a good idea following Dad's passing for her to escape the heat of summer and return to Wisconsin to be close to my brothers and their families. I agreed to check on her house while she was away. About a week after Mom left, I checked on her house. When I walked in, I realized this was the first time I had been alone in their house since Dad died. I felt an overwhelming sense of loss. Everywhere I looked, I thought of him. I walked into the den and saw his recliner and visualized Dad as he was during those last terrible months when he had been so sick.

I felt an urgency to sit in his chair. As I sat down, closed my eyes, and put my head back, I could feel Dad with me, and the image of him being frail and sick seemed to wash away. My loneliness subsided as I remembered our past together. I was filled with beautiful memories of the two of us: when I was three years old and Dad's big strong arms saved me from drowning in the ocean in Florida; those same strong arms later taught me how to swim so I would not fear the water. I remembered him walking the floors with me when I was a child with chronic earaches. I remembered how proud I was of my strong Daddy as he did his special dives off the diving board. I remembered that he made sure I got the puppy I so desperately wanted for my eighth birthday, and how he cried just as hard as I did when my puppy died some months later. I remembered waiting for him in the front yard (with my new dog) to come home from work or the golf course so I could tell him all the wonderful things that had happened that day. I remembered the long hours when the two of us would go fishing, and how we fought off the mosquitoes, Dad would laugh at me for insisting that we name our live bait.

I also remembered all the other fun times when he would make me laugh and how he taught me that laughter heals. I remembered working alongside him at his dental office each summer during high school and college, and often how he would tell me how proud he was of me, and how proud I was of him for the compassion he had for his patients.

I remembered how I cherished our long rides home from work as he told me things, such as our family history and what boys to be careful of and why I should be home from dates at a reasonable hour. I remembered that when he forgave me for many indiscretions, this taught me to love unconditionally. Everyone cared about him and respected him, and he and Mom had a beautiful loving relationship and set a wonderful example for me. I remembered the special father-daughter relationship we had and how proud I was to have him as my Dad. Most of all, I remembered that he taught me to love and how to share my love.

I desperately wanted to know that my Dad was safe, that he was living and happy. I wanted to know if he could see me and if he was still a part of my life. Most of all, I wanted to know whether our love had survived his physical death. As I opened my eyes, the room was as still and as empty as before. I had a long-overdue cry, then I laughed at myself for being so foolish. However, I still wanted some sign from Dad that he was with me. My memories were keeping him alive in my heart, but I wanted to be able to feel his presence.

I do not know what I expected. Sitting in his chair brought all of these wonderful memories. That should have been enough. But selfishly, I wanted more—something, anything—but nothing happened. Reluctantly, I finished checking the house and left.

I sat in my car for a few minutes, waiting for the engine to cool off. I normally don't turn the radio on while driving, because I enjoy the quiet time to think, contemplate, and reflect. For some reason, that day I turned the radio on. As I listened, I instantly knew that Dad was with me, that love truly does survive physical death, and in fact, that there is no such thing as death. Death died for me that day. You see, the song that "happened" to be playing on the radio was "You'll Always Be My Baby!" A song we often listened to together. Thanks, Dad, I love you too.

Mary Christner

The Rose

I believe that if you open your heart and mind, you can receive signs from God on a regular basis. It is also my belief that until you have extraordinary experiences of your own, it is hard to relate to and appreciate the stories of others. My experiences started after losing some instrumental people in my life.

My experience was one that I found miraculous and healing. I received a message on April 23 from an uncle in upstate New York. I was surprised, for although I come from a tight and very close family, it is rare that I receive calls from relatives outside my immediate family, for we are all geographically distanced. I immediately knew that someone in my family must have passed on, but I never in a million years thought it could be one of my cousins. I thought for sure it would be an aunt or uncle, for I am the second youngest of sixteen cousins and most of our parents are in their sixties and early seventies.

Unfortunately, I learned on that morning that I am now the youngest living cousin. My younger cousin had taken his life. While I try to keep everyone I know and love close to my heart, I am guilty of spacing some people out every once in a while. I thought it was ironic that I had actually been thinking about Joey during most of my morning commute.

It was only a few months earlier that I was elated to learn that our family was going to have a reunion, but saddened to hear that Joey would not attend. I immediately called him and told him that it wouldn't be a party without him. Unfortunately, Joey was going through some pretty difficult marital problems at the time and just didn't feel up to attending. It is not unlike me to pick up the phone and call someone I normally do not keep in touch with, so I didn't think much of it.

After learning of Joey's death, I got into my car and the first song that came on the radio was "Thank You for Being My Friend," immediately followed by "Only the Good Die Young." It seems that I am constantly being given signs that have significant meanings. I wondered if my last phone call had meant more to Joey than a simple hello. I didn't learn until many months later from his mom that he had been very appreciative of my call.

Not long after Joey's death, the beginning of a very interesting two months began, as we drove through the hills of New York State on an early April morning. I spent most of the time thinking and praying as I stared out the car window. What I saw from my window was comforting. There was a two-story home with a sliding glass door, and the moisture on the door formed a perfect image of the Blessed Mother. My immediate thought was that Joey was going to be okay. I didn't mention anything to my aunt, uncle, or cousin with whom I was traveling. My belief was that this was a sign from Heaven and I was meant to see it. I thought, "Maybe I just saw what I wanted to see." It wasn't until later that I realized this was more than a coincidence.

Approximately one month after Joey's death, we lost another person who was deeply loved by hundreds of people. No man could ever fill my dad's shoes, but this one came close. I loved him with the same respect and honor that I loved my own dad. Monsignor Gorski was bigger than life in my eyes, and much more than a friend. He baptized, married, and eulogized almost all of my family members. He wasn't only there for the good times; he helped us through the difficult periods, in a way that no other human could have. We knew for months that the reality of losing Monsignor in the near future was real.

As I drove home from work on a Monday night, I could not escape the strong aroma of my father. This is something that I experience every now and then. I felt that I had to send Monsignor a card expressing my love and appreciation to him before he was also gone. I felt that my dad's presence was a sign that I'd better move quickly. I mailed my card Tuesday morning, hoping that the Monsignor would get it before it was too late.

My dreams come true on many occasions, for I feel as if I am sometimes given messages based on future events. On Thursday morning, I awoke from a very interesting dream. The essence of this dream was that I must stop running from my feelings and let people know how important they are to me. After reviewing my dream and thinking about how significant it was, I received a phone call from my sister. The news that I dreaded so deeply had arrived. Monsignor Gorski had died, and he hadn't received my card. If I hadn't sent the card, I don't think that I could have ever forgiven myself. The simple fact that I had tried made a world of difference to me. Did my earlier dream have more significance than I initially realized?

I experienced intense emotions on Thursday. I didn't like or understand some of the emotions (e.g., anger) but they were there, and I could not run from them. I guess that I was in shock because Monsignor Gorski's death did not affect me fully for a number of days. A few oddities occurred, but nothing compared to what soon followed.

It started on Friday night, when I decided that I had to send a dozen roses for the funeral service. I called two aunts on Saturday to get information regarding florists in the area. I left a message for Aunt Jane and I also spoke to Aunt Helen. Aunt Helen told me that it had been requested that nobody send flowers. There would be too many people at Mass and they could not fit any floral arrangements in the church. Again, Monsignor was a beloved priest and friend to so many people, and the church could not accommodate the expected crowds.

Later that day, I returned to my apartment and received a message from both of my aunts. Aunt Helen's message stated that I was instructed to deliver the flowers to the altar of the Blessed Mother. Aunt Jane told me who to call and what to say in order to have the flower arrangement done for Monsignor Gorski. How could I have my flowers delivered to the altar of the Blessed Mother? That would be too much of an honor for a regular girl like myself, and why was I given permission from a total stranger to do this? After giving it a lot of thought, I decided that I had played no part in this instruction, so it must have been meant to be. I was later told that there were only three flower arrangements standing by the Blessed Mother: one from the May crowning, one from the Rosary Confraternity, and one from me.

The funeral would take place Tuesday morning. It was as if I hit a brick wall on Monday. As the day progressed, my mental and physical conditions diminished. At one point, I felt as if I would snap. I was apprehensive about being alone, but who would understand the pain and loss that I was feeling? My family loved this man as much as I did, so I didn't want to turn to them, adding to their own grief. I prayed all night and again in the morning.

Tuesday was a very gloomy and cloudy day. My last thought before getting out of my car was, "God, Monsignor Gorski, and Dad, please help me get through this because I can't do it on my own." As I took a step away from my car, a sharp light caught the corner of my left eye. I wondered why the streetlights in the parking lot were still on. I looked over my left shoulder and had the most incredible experience of my life.

The light was coming from the sky. It was the brightest and warmest light that I had ever seen or experienced. I felt as if I were an open sore and that I had been healed. When a co-worker came in a few minutes later, she stated that the sky was black outside and it looked like we were in for some rain. I knew at that moment that the light I had seen was more than a break in the clouds. As the day progressed, my experiences sank in more and more. I lay in bed that night and thought about the difference in feeling I had experienced over the last twenty-four-hour period. There was no comparison. It was incredible.

All of a sudden, everything hit me—the image of the Blessed Mother, the inescapable desire to send roses to my special angel, the placement of the roses, the significance of my dream, the sky opening immediately after my prayer. In addition, one of my closest friends, for whom my father had a great love, delivered a baby on April 23 and named her Bianca Rose. It never crossed my mind that a rose signifies the Blessed Mother, but after this experience, the rose will never leave my mind. It was on that special day that for me death died.

Lauralee Koziol

The Dairy Queen

As I own and operate an angel store, my mother and I went to the Angel Collector's Club Convention in Kansas City in September 1997. One night while we were sleeping, my mother suddenly woke me up and said, "What time is it?" I looked at the clock: it was 4:44 A.M.

The next year in April, my mother was diagnosed with stage four pancreatic cancer. A few nights after we learned this horrible news, I woke up at 4:44 A.M. with the message that my mother was going to be okay, that this was a test of faith. I knew in my heart that whether my mother lived or passed on, she would be okay. After that, whenever I would wake up at 4:44, I would just say, "Thank you," and lie there and wait for the message to come through.

Miraculously, my mother lived for a year with her cancer. During that time I did automatic writing of poetry, something I had never done before. Her cancer was very painful, but she was able to remain at home, as my father was her primary caregiver and she had the aid of hospice. For the last week of her life, I slept on the sofa in the living room. Early one morning around five-thirty, she woke up screaming, "I'm dying! I'm dying!" I heard my father say, "What?"

When I got into their room, she was sitting up. She started speaking in tongues. I said to my dad, "She's speaking in tongues. This is amazing!" I thought that maybe this was going to be her last day with us, so I insisted that my dad call some of our relatives who I felt needed to be able to say good-bye to her.

We got her into her wheelchair and made her presentable. She was still able to say things like, "Thank you for coming." During the afternoon, my son Kyle, who is thirty, finally stopped by. At that point, Mom was no longer able to carry on any kind of conversation, although she did say very clearly, "I'm going home." I answered, "Yes, you are Mom, it's okay." After that she never said anything again that I could understand.

During her final week with us, I was very tired one night and fell asleep very early. By then, Mom was sleeping in a hospital bed in the spare bedroom. I woke up about five-thirty A.M. and went in to check on her.

My walking across the floor woke up my dad. I told him I was going to go home since everything seemed to be all right. He told me later that he heard me shut the door but did not hear me drive away. So he figured he fell asleep right away. Then, fifteen minutes later, he rolled over and looked at the clock. Then he looked at the doorway of his bedroom and saw an image of someone standing there. When I asked him to describe it, he said it was not white and transparent, but a darker color, almost a type of copper. It was such a vivid image that he got up and walked around the house to see if someone had gotten inside after I had left. He also told me later that when he tried to fall asleep, he had felt a hand and fingers press against his shoulder as if someone were trying to help him calm down. We don't know if he was visited by an angel or by Mom, her spirit being out of her body, but whatever it was, it was comforting to both of us to know that we weren't alone. Mom passed away peacefully with grace and dignity several days later.

Almost immediately after Mom's passing, I started receiving what I consider to be signs from her that she was not very far away. She first came to me in a dream and said she was worried about the checkbook. Since she always balanced the checkbook, I told Dad the next day that he needed to balance it because Mom was worried about it.

Then I started getting signs of Dairy Queen trash. Mom loved the DQ and the minister had said at her funeral that if Dorothy had one fault, it was that she loved the Dairy Queen. He said that whenever their travels took them to a new town, she was always able to spot the red roof of the DQ.

After the funeral, my cousin and I stopped for a memorial ice cream cone, and I put the napkin and trash into my purse and forgot about it. About a week later, I was delivering memorial checks to the American Cancer Society and I noticed on the bottom step outside the building a piece of trash that was a sundae cup from Dairy Queen. I just said, "Thanks, Mom, I needed that!" Then I laughed about it all day. A few days later, I was at the post office and I was digging in my purse for a pen, and out popped a napkin from the Dairy Queen. At first, this freaked me out because I had forgotten that my cousin and I had gone to the DQ after Mom's funeral and I had thrown the trash into my purse.

A few days later, my girlfriend Arla and I were on a shopping spree, and we decided to do some comparison shopping for baby clothes, since she was a new grandma. We were heading for the Half Price Store and all of a sudden Arla said, "Why don't we go to Wal-Mart instead?"

I said that was fine and we headed for Wal-Mart (one of Mom's favorite stores). It was about ten P.M. when we were coming out of the store to the car, and I noticed a napkin on the pavement with the red logo of the Dairy Queen. (Thanks, Mom!) Of course, there were no Dairy Queens anywhere near any of these locations. There have been numerous other sightings of Dairy Queen trash that I won't go into because I think you get the picture. Dad feels left out, because even though he always drove Mom to DQ, he hasn't been getting any of the messages like I have. I'm sure Mom is sending him signs he just can't figure out yet.

Easter Poem

My mother is living with cancer this year,
Showing lots of courage and nothing to fear.
The days can be long and full of tests,
Now we've made it to Easter and know we've been blessed.
It's been a year since the diagnosis was heard,
We're not really sure if she'll ever be cured.
But Dad is ever watchful at her side,
Giving her pills and taking it all in stride.
He protects her and takes care of her in every way,
Filled with new strength from God every day.
Faith plays a big part of the overall plan,
You can do anything your heart says you can.
Please join us as we give thanks and pray,
"Thank you, God, for each and every new day."

4-3-99

Dorothy's Going Home

Her name is Dorothy and we all loved her so,
She wanted to stay but knew it was her time to go.
The last few words we understood her to say,
Were "I'm going home," but it wasn't that day.
I answered her, "Yes you are, Mom, go to the Light,"
I'm sure she had our Lord clear in her sight.
Angels came and showed her the way,
She was at peace when she left us that day.
I thought I was through crying until the shock set in,
Then a flood of tears came out again.
I know she's watching me from above,
Sending me lots of comfort and love.
Now I'll try to stop crying again,
I'm waiting for her to send me a sign when she's all settled in.
We're not really so very far apart,
Because those we love will always be in our heart.

4-27-99

Karen Montague

The Chimes

I am writing about the death of loved ones. It concerns a phone call I received from my daughter about something that happened to my granddaughter in August of 1999.

Twenty-one years ago, my daughter was married to Michael, and they had a daughter named Heather. When Heather was eighteen months old, Michael was killed on a motorcycle. My daughter was only nineteen at the time, and was numb for about a year and a half. Their marriage had not been working well, and they were separated at the time of his death. My daughter functioned, but it took a long time for her to even cry and grieve his passing. She said he appeared to her from time to time in dreams and that she could often feel him around her.

This last August, Heather told her mother she was lying in bed reading when she heard one of the chimes in her room start chiming. She said the windows were closed, no fans were running, and the air conditioner was off. She ignored it, but about fifteen minutes later, it began chiming again. She thought her husband was playing a trick, but after checking the driveway, she found he had gone to work. This went on for forty-five minutes, and then stopped. Later in the day, she went to visit her grandmother, Michael's mother, and told her the story. Her grandmother said, "Oh, that was just your dad coming around to say hello. He died twenty-one years ago today."

Marilyn Fernandez

The Eagles

In August of 1992, I left my beloved brother Roger, fifty-six years old, in intensive care and kissed him good-bye, assuring myself that he would recover. Then my husband and I began our usual two-month vacation. I would call every three days to check on Roger.

On Saturday morning, I called the ICU and spoke with my daughter Patty, and was told Roger would not make it through the following twelve hours. I was devastated. Here I was in Bozeman, Montana, some thousand miles away, wanting desperately to be with my brother to comfort him. I remembered Roger told me years ago he once almost died and started going through a tunnel, but he had been afraid and refused to go into it.

My thoughtful daughter put the phone up to my brother's ear. As I fought back the sobs, I struggled for words to reassure him not to be afraid. I told him to go to the Light, and that we would all be together someday. Roger could not speak because of the life-support tubes, but he acknowledged to Patty that he understood. We cried together over the phone. I told him that I loved him and would miss him very much. I feel so fortunate to have called at that particular time to comfort him so he would not be afraid, as well as to say good-bye to my beloved brother.

An hour later as we sat down for breakfast, I felt a wonderful, overwhelming feeling of love, peace, and calmness. I heard a loud voice within my head saying, "Everything is okay." This voice felt so natural, like it was a part of me, reassuring and comforting me. I knew then that my dear brother had made it okay to the Other Side, and that he passed on at the same time I heard the voice. I am so grateful for this feeling and for my inner voice, which actually started me on my spiritual quest.

We drove as fast as we could towards home. That Saturday night, we stopped at Kennewick, Washington. All the motels were full because of a weekend event, except for a newly opened motel called the Silver Cloud Inn, where we spent the night. How amazing!

After I arrived home in Eureka, California, my daughter and I were making funeral arrangements and decided to use an eagle design on the memorandum cards. We agreed that Roger would love using the eagle, being that he was an ex-marine and had also served in the army. During the viewing of my brother's body, the funeral home played "Beautiful Dreamer" and another tune, both of which were our mother's favorites. I felt she was also with us in spirit.

After the funeral, we continued our much-needed vacation. From the moment we left home, eagles came constantly across my path during our travels. For example, we saw signs and motel names having the word "eagle" in them and eagle car license plates. Everything was eagle, even sculptures of eagles with the artists' names being the same as my brother's first name, another with his last name, and yet another with our father's first name, Sherman.

My daughter also experienced many eagle signs. While in Roger's house, the moment she turned on the television, an eagle in flight turned its head and looked at her.

But the most awesome eagle experience occurred when we were viewing a laser light show that was projected against the wall of the great Grand Coulee Dam, the dam my father helped build in the 1930s. The show was projecting an eagle soaring across the wall towards a fish. Then, the show suddenly quit, stopped dead. The projectionist apologized and said in all the six years of the show this had never happened before. Fifteen minutes later, that same scene of the eagle soaring toward the fish was repeated. I believe without any doubt that my father and mother were letting me know that Roger was with them and that he was okay. I felt so thankful. It changed my life. Our eagle events continued for two months, then became fewer and finally ended.

We are so grateful and blessed for these experiences. These are miracles from Heaven. We thank our loved ones who are in the spirit world so very much.

Patricia Cloyd

There are more clairvoyants living today than in any other time in history. This is not an accident. It is because of the spiritual consciousness that is spreading throughout the entire world, like never before in the history of mankind. —In God's Truth

Lifting the Veil

My father, who by profession was a film director and producer, had an interest in the paranormal. He created, wrote, produced, and directed a television series in 1958 entitled *The Veil*. It was based on actual case studies of paranormal occurrences; e.g., people being contacted by ghosts from the Other Side. Boris Karloff hosted and starred in each episode, which was presented in a mysterious, chilling manner with eerie music.

Unfortunately, Hal Roach Studios, where my father worked and produced this series, went bankrupt. *The Veil* was shelved and never released. Shortly thereafter, the popular Alfred Hitchcock series aired and remained successful for a long time, although Hitchcock's stories were not actual cases. Because of the bankruptcy, my father, very frustrated, could never claim his work, and it remained in the studio archives.

Years later, I attempted to sell the series for my father to some foreign television stations. My father had access to some of the original reels for a couple of the episodes. However, at the time, there was a reduction of foreign purchases of American-made programs. All I can say is, it came to no a-veil.

My father led a full life and had an exciting career making films and videos. He even won an Oscar for best documentary in 1961, but I know *The Veil* was a frustration for him. He succumbed to prostate cancer in October 1997, at the age of eighty. Four months prior to his passing, my grandmother also decided to pass over. Five months after my father's passing, my husband's mother had made a similar decision. We had already lost my mother and his father approximately ten years previously. So within one year, we lost the last of two generations between our two families. Nothing like getting it all over with at once. Somehow you know it's not really final, you'll meet again; but then you can't help feeling at times like a middle-aged orphan.

On Father's Day, eight months after my father's departure, we were at the beach with my two daughters. The day was glorious and the water crystal clear. It was a perfect day at the beach. An elderly man, perhaps in his late seventies, began conversing with the girls while we were splashing around. He showed them some live conch shells and took an interest in the girls even though he was there with his own young grandson and his wife.

After a while, I rinsed off at the shower, and on my way back, I stopped on the boardwalk to bask in the sun and inhale the great aromas of the beach. Closing my eyes, I started to feel nostalgic and then it dawned on me that I was on the beach to which my father had introduced me, and it was the first Father's Day of my life without him. Suddenly, I felt his presence on that beach.

When I got back to my beach towel, the elderly gentleman approached me to say how proud I should be of my two girls. He said they were delightful and beautiful, and while one was very smart, the other had the twinkle of the

devil in her eye. I knew he meant these comments endear-
ingly. He had captured their essences in such a short time. I
asked him if he was vacationing, and he said that he lived
full-time in a gated community two towns away. It happened
to be the same place my father had lived, but they had never
known each other. The man expressed a liking for my girls
and was very grandfatherly towards them. It was a strange
coincidence, almost surreal but very pleasant.

A few weeks later, a front-page article in a local newspaper I rarely read caught my eye on the rack while I was in
the supermarket. It was about a local video producer who
had had an unusual experience with a medium from New
York. The medium could communicate with people on the
Other Side and pass helpful messages to their living loved
ones. My initial interest in the article was due to the fact that
I was looking for a video production company to collabo-
rate with on a few of my marketing projects. However, I
have to admit, the "Other Side" part of it was intriguing,
since I had been thinking about my father a lot at that time,
and the kids and I had started dreaming about him with
more frequency. The dreams were amusing: my father sitting down for dinner in front of a plate piled high with
assorted jelly beans (his favorite snack), or my father playing
hide-and-seek with my youngest daughter.

I met with the video producer. He told me the story of
how strange and coincidental his project was with the medium, John Edwards. He stated that he didn't believe in this
sort of thing, but felt compelled to approach him at a semi-
nar to offer his services. The medium said that he had been
waiting for him even though they didn't know each other.
The two of them spent six months working together and
produced a set of videos, which were subsequently sent to
Larry King. Shortly thereafter, Larry King asked Edwards to
be a guest on his show. It was a major success. The phones
were ringing off the hook, and he's been asked back several
times since.

The videotapes, which the producer gave me to review,

consisted of footage of Edwards's workshops, and showed him providing incredibly accurate information about people whom he couldn't possibly have known. One of the tapes was an instructional video on how to read the symbols and signals that your loved ones send from the Other Side. Apparently, they hide things or play around with electronics, light bulbs, machinery, and telephones. Ever notice how a radio, television, or telephone, without warning, goes haywire and then for no apparent reason starts to work again? Well, guess what? According to Edwards, it could be a relative fooling around or trying to get your attention. Our loved ones also come to us vividly in our dreams.

One night, my sister called me around midnight. She had just gotten back from the house of an acquaintance from work who happened to be a psychic. She had initially gone there for a reading about her personal life. In the middle of the reading, my father barged in to make his presence known. He was accompanied by my mother and uncle, but his energy was so strong, he overpowered the other two. My sister told me the psychic wanted me to call her in the morning because my father had much to tell me. She was amazed because he sent airplanes and helicopters over the house to ensure everyone knew he was there. The woman's dog was barking hysterically throughout the reading.

The next morning, I called the psychic. She was exhausted, and asked me if I could hear the commotion. Her dog was barking, and it sounded like airplanes were flying low overhead. All night long, she had been kept awake by this noise. My father had essentially moved in with her and had instructed her to watch a movie on television at two A.M., but she didn't understand the film. His message to me was that it was imperative that I watch this same movie, *Smilla's Sense of Snow*, and that I needed more "moxie." I can say this was true about me at that time, because I always felt I was at a low level of energy. The thoroughly exhausted psychic had to get ready for work and asked me to call her at lunchtime to continue the conversation. Unfortunately, it was the last time I ever talked with her again. She quit her job that day and she never returned the numerous phone calls both my sister and I left for her. Maybe Dad was a little overbearing.

Imagine the frustration that my father felt, since the psychic abandoned us in midstream, especially since he wasn't a very patient man, at least when he had been alive. I decided to call a woman in town who did this sort of thing. She agreed to help us out, but we would have to wait a week before she could schedule us. As we were talking, the phone line started crackling very loudly, and she mentioned that, yes indeed, my father was a strong-willed soul and would have to learn some patience. She also explained that the previous psychic had not learned to establish her boundaries, so my father took over her house and yes, she had flipped out. I felt sorry for this woman. The crackling sound I heard was my father trying to barge in on our conversation.

After I hung up, I laughed and found myself talking into the air to my father. I berated him for barging in on that poor woman and told him he needed to be more patient. I told him to rest assured that one way or another, I would make sure he got his message to me. As I walked through the living room, something on the floor caught my eye. Stooping to pick it up, I realized it was a small sticker (belonging to no one in the house, because I asked them all later) with a happy face on it. I burst out laughing. You see, the happy face was my father's hallmark. He signed every letter and greeting card with a happy face next to his name. He stuck it on all fan switches in his house to differentiate them from regular light switches. Here it was, on my floor, as if he were signaling that he was relieved and happy about my promise.

Throughout the following week, as we waited patiently for the appointment, airplanes and helicopters began circling the house. One helicopter hovered outside my living room window for about three minutes on one occasion. Mind you, we are not on any flight path, and helicopters had never flown over our house so frequently before. The first psychic had low-flying aircraft problems the night my dad "moved in" with her. Here he was again. My father had been a pilot during the Second World War—he flew 106 missions in addition to D-Day, so flying was a passion for him.

Another symbol from my father started to appear—frogs, particularly a real one that hung out by our front door, looking through the window. It later would appear on special occasions like birthdays and Christmas, or when I was upset about something, as if the frog were trying to comfort me. Frogs were significant to my father. Before he died, he had me paint a picture of a crane trying to swallow a frog. The frog clutches the bird's throat, choking it, preventing himself from being swallowed. The caption reads, "Don't ever give up!"

Finally, the appointed day for the psychic reading arrived. The session was conducted by telephone for an hour. Essentially, my father was trying to show me what it was like on the Other Side. He was having a lot of fun exhibiting his new talents. The movie he wanted me to watch (*Smilla's Sense of Snow*) would show me that I should be aware of my own intuitive/psychic self. (I am clairvoyant, but didn't know it at the time.) He said that I should be discerning as I discover more about the true reality, and I should never give up, like the frog in the crane's mouth.

Dad said that I should learn to channel so that I could open up more and connect with spirit. He was excited to show me what he was experiencing on the other side of the veil. My world was changing fast and more was to come. The psychic saw that I was about to go through some enormous changes through a type of spiritual aerobics. She suggested that I pace myself, get centered, go to the beach, listen to music, be loving to myself, and get rid of negatives. The ride was about to begin. It sounded exciting, and I was amazed how strongly my father was coming through to tell me all this. It was as if he were on the sidelines doing jumping jacks to get my attention, and he was making me laugh.

One night a short time later, my husband told me that

John Edwards was on Larry King Live again. He was taking calls from viewers and putting people in touch with their loved ones on the other side. My husband and I thought it would be a kick to call in to see if my father would come through. I put out a cosmic message to him and called. Unfortunately, we couldn't get through, but we continued watching. Edwards was connecting with each caller with amazing accuracy. Then, a caller from Denmark asked about his relative and Edwards said that he was getting pilot symbols. He asked him if this relative was a pilot. The man paused and said no, that he had no pilots in his family. Edwards kept insisting that a pilot was coming through and apologized to the caller. My husband and I looked at each other and laughed. We both knew Dad had barged his way through again.

At the end of October 1998, my brother called from California to let me know that a writer from New York had contacted him via the Internet. He wanted to write an article on my father and the television series that he had created in 1958. Naturally, he was talking about *The Veil*.

My brother gave him my number, since I was the keeper of the family records. I had some information on *The Veil* from the files my father left and a copy of one of the episodes on video. The writer called and informed me that the entire series was being sold as a three-tape video set—all ten episodes would be packaged together. He had seen it advertised in a magazine and decided to write about it. Apparently, someone had retrieved them from a warehouse (and hopefully obtained the rights) and was selling them on the open market. The writer, who freelances for monster magazines, was interested in the Boris Karloff aspect of the series.

I called the company in Washington that was selling the videos to order the set. The moment they arrived, I watched them all. Some of the stories were tucked away in my childhood memory banks, others I didn't remember at all. But one thing was certain: my father was the creator and producer for all of them, and the director for one. I sent some information to the writer along with pictures. The fifty-page article was published in a monster magazine one year later. Curiously, upon learning the date of my father's death, the writer was intrigued by the fact that it was exactly one year later to the day (October 16, 1998) that he had gotten the idea to write the article on *The Veil* and search for my father.

The key point to all of this is both the title of the series, *The Veil*, and the subject matter. All episodes were true stories about people having strange experiences with ghosts and entities from the Other Side. This was exactly what my father was trying to accomplish with me. It seemed as though he wanted me to peek through the veil and share with him the truths he had found and I had forgotten. Before the writer sent his article off to be published, he asked me to write his closing paragraph. This is what I wrote:

His daughter Barbara believes her father would be pleased to know that *The Veil* has resurfaced. It must have been frustrating for him to work hard on the series only to have it never get farther than a dusty old archive. Where it ended up certainly wasn't intended, but at least something good came out of it—a video series and this very informative article. He's probably smiling about this up in heaven . . . or, who knows, behind that veil!

I love you, Dad. This one's for you and for all those who can gain insight and comfort from our story. God bless you.

Barbara Bibas Montero

Beloved Ashley

It all started in November when a very close friend of mine asked what I wanted as a birthday gift. I responded, "Nothing. I don't need a thing." I jokingly added, "Maybe flowers. I love flowers and I don't receive them often."

He persisted, "Surely there is something you want." I told him, "I would love to see the group M People in concert." He informed me that they do not perform here in the United States. My response was, "So?" Within a week, we had booked tickets complete with backstage passes to London for the final night of their tour.

We departed for England on Thursday morning, December 17, 1998. We arrived in London on Friday morning, having had no sleep. We had talked all the way through the layover in New York, through the trip to London, and through the breakfast at the hotel. The room was not ready, so we went out for a walk that lasted all day and night. We headed back to the hotel at four A.M. Saturday morning, but found the Tower record store was still open. As we are both in the music industry, how could we resist?

We entered the store, and after about ten minutes, I felt very weak, such that I could not explain the feeling. I told my friend, "We have to leave now!" I did not know what was happening. I felt so strange. I could not walk the few blocks back to the hotel. We got a taxi and were back to the hotel in minutes. I told my friend that I wanted to get a soda from the store next door to the hotel. He responded, "I'll go up to the room. Would you get me something too?"

When I entered the hotel room again, I heard him say. "Oh my God, this can't be happening. . . . Oh, God. Yes, Eric is walking in right now." It was my brother on the phone. He was calling to say my only son, Ashley, had been rushed to the hospital from his job. He had had a cardiac arrest and had not recovered from CPR, and they were transferring him to Birmingham, Alabama, for a heart transplant. Needless to say, with no sleep, jet lag, and news like that, I was not able to process the information very well. I could not believe that my twenty-one-year-old son was in such trouble. Within the next thirty minutes, more phone calls came in, each one with more bad news. I began to pray and tried to communicate with my son. I locked myself up in the bathroom and cried and prayed. I asked God what was happening. Why was this going on? Why my only son? Why so young? Why?

Through my tears came the answer. God told me, "Your son has returned Home." At that very moment, I could feel my son. I felt as though he were with me in London. I could smell him. I felt his love, his warmth, everything but his physical person.

I don't remember much about the trip home, except the cab driver who hugged me when I got to the airport in London to return to the U.S. I remember the flight attendant who sat next to me from New York to Atlanta, and my mother's face when I departed the plane in Birmingham. She told me that they had pronounced Ashley dead only eight hours earlier.

During the next few days, I found it very difficult to control my emotions. It had been only five days earlier that I had held my son in my arms and told him how much I loved him. He had never been sick. We did not expect anything like this to happen. I was in shock.

My ex-wife informed me that she had agreed to an autopsy. I asked her why. I knew they would find nothing. I knew it was that God had called his angel Home. I knew this with all my heart. I knew the entire time while traveling home that Ashley had left us. I could feel it. I trusted in God that he had Ashley in His Light. When I could no longer control my emotional state, I would cry hysterically for a minute or two, then a peace would come over me such as I had never experienced before. I would become calm and at ease. It was unbelievable. During the services and the weeks afterwards, this calmness would come over me. I knew it was Ashley's spirit.

It has been nearly seven months since my son's passing. It has been difficult not to be able to see him, touch him, hold him, tell him how much I love him—so very hard. I know these are emotions we experience because we are in the physical plane. I continue to pray for answers. During one of my talks with God, I asked what is it I am supposed to learn from all of this. I prayed for His help to understand my lessons. His reply has kept me at peace. "Just as you love your son, so do I love my son, and as I love you, my son." These words have repeated themselves over and over in my mind. I had not imagined that God loved me so much.

I say to all of you, especially those with children, love them as God loves them. Love them as God loves you, and always know that God does love you.

I go through each day missing my son. It is never easy. It is still the same that I am here and he is not. But just as we learn to communicate with each other in this world, we must also learn to communicate with each other in the spiritual world. "Pay attention" is what I hear over and over.

I have been paying attention, and often I feel Ashley is around me. There are so many signs that his spirit is near. It is such a comfort. I know he is with God in love and peace. I hope these words might comfort someone who has lost a child or someone very dear to them. I pray for comfort for all of you who live with such a loss. Know that your loved one is with God and that God loves them.

Eric DeLaune

The Spiritual Signs

I was drowning in my sadness. I grabbed an afghan and lay down on the couch. "If I close my eyes, I can shut out the world," I thought. It was midday. But the next day, it was the same, and the next day and the next. I arose in the mornings feeling life was useless. "What does it matter what I do? Life is not worth living." These thoughts went through my head over and over again.

My husband had died suddenly, such that I kept telling myself, "I can't believe he is gone." Don could not breathe in those last two weeks without a respirator. He had been diagnosed with a lung disease that was not curable and for which the medical world did not even know the cause. He did not suffer long and I was thankful for that, but he was only sixty-one years old. I kept asking myself, "Why did he have to go now, when we had just retired early to enjoy life?"

A week after my husband died, our dog, Wags, decided not to eat any longer. She became so weak that I had to have her put to sleep. Two losses within a week! My burden was heavy. I cried often. I lost thirty pounds within a few months. Food had no appeal. Living had no appeal.

My sister and brother-in-law would invite me to go shopping or to their home for dinner. Phone calls, cards, and letters of sympathy poured in, but it was always the same whenever I was home—I was alone. Six months passed like this, then the "happenings" started.

I invited my sister and brother-in-law for dinner. My sister was helping me in the kitchen when we were both startled to hear a dog barking within a few feet of us. Its voice sounded muffled. "Maybe Don is having Wags speak," my sister said. Little did I know I was about to embark upon a new experience in my life.

The next event occurred one morning upon returning home from grocery shopping. I entered the house and heard a buzzer. It was the oven timer, but as I had not used the oven for months, I wondered if Don was nearby.

A few days later, I was in the kitchen and thought I heard the doorbell, but it seemed quieter than normal. I peered out the front door, but no one was there. However, I was startled to see exquisite light coming from behind a tall fir tree. The rays of light were forming a star-like prism. It was beautiful! Was Don trying to share this with me? I would not have seen it if I had not "thought" I heard the doorbell.

Then, perfume began to fill the air, perfume like my mother used to wear. This was followed by either cigarette smoke or pipe tobacco. My dad in his earlier years smoked cigarettes, and my grandfather always preferred a pipe. They have both passed on.

Another day, after a strong windstorm, I decided to clean the gutters on our huge carport. Between the carport and an adjoining fence, there is just enough room to place the feet of the ladder. As I was extending the top of the ladder, I tripped over some blackberry vines. Ladder in hand, and falling, I braced myself to soften the brunt of the fall. Instead, I felt a gentle hand catch me and stand me and the ladder back upright until I regained my balance. It had to be a spiritual intervention. No one else was around, and the ladder was heavy.

The beautiful aromas continued, and sometimes it was funny. One day, I decided to try adopting a dog that was advertised in the newspaper. Buddy was a small white dog with a dark brown circle around one eye. I loved him, but he couldn't get along with my kitty, so I had to return him. One night, he got up on all fours on the bed facing the pillows, and began sniffing around, raising his head up and down to sniff the air. I leaned on my elbow and smelled perfume and tobacco for at least thirty seconds. "I am glad you smell it too," I told the little doggy. I have also smelled cake and Jell-O, and one morning I smelled coffee brewing as I came down the stairs. I am not a coffee drinker, but my husband had a coffeepot on every morning.

One day, I was looking through boxes for an album that contained information about my grandmother and grandfather. I was surprised to smell a different perfume this time (it was the same familiar pipe tobacco aroma) and I imagined they must be looking through the album with me. I sometimes experience a different, almost Victorian perfume welcoming me in the mornings, also with intermittent cigarette smoke. Could it be my great-grandparents? I had an aunt who loved to watch Lawrence Welk on television and who had used a perfume with a hint of orange scent. I turned on the television one evening and was delighted to see a performance of Lawrence Welk from about twenty years ago. I began to smell orange-scented perfume! I wasn't thinking of my family at that particular moment, but they were obviously thinking of me.

There are other "happenings" too. When I work on a crossword puzzle, I sometimes feel the pen move by itself, filling in the letters. Don enjoyed crossword puzzles. Sometimes the bathroom door is slightly closed when I know I have left it open and the cat is not in the house to push it closed. Sometimes I hear the metal tags of a dog collar rattling. My two deceased dogs always woke us up in the mornings by shaking their collars. They are now in "doggy heaven" and yet they are with me.

I will never get over missing Don and my family, but I now know that one day I will join them with great joy. They show me that. Even though I can't see them, they are often with me. I feel that the real purpose in life is learning to love one another. With that in mind, I ask myself, "What can I do that is nice for someone today?" I am humbled that my spirit family keeps me company from time to time. I am blessed and grateful.

Doris Christensen

God Himself and Herself cannot be seen, but only experienced. It is impossible for us, in our human form, to truly see God. But we can experience God in every moment of our lives, through everything that we can see, feel, hear, and touch that is good, that brings us happiness, joy, serenity, peace, pleasure and comfort, for it is a manifestation of God.
—In God's Truth

Whoosh

I have walked with death twice in my life. Both times, I was vividly aware of the spirit leaving the material body.

In the spring of 1946, I was fifteen and standing beside my father's bed at two A.M. in the parlor of our house. The parlor had been converted into a makeshift sickroom. Back then, when one had heart disease, one didn't get out of bed, never mind climb the stairs to the bedroom or walk to the kitchen. After a couple weeks in the hospital, the parlor was the final resting place for my father. Mother, a registered nurse, slept on a cot beside the bed.

Mother's loud call up the stairs awakened me, and by the time I reached the parlor, she was in the kitchen trying to sterilize a syringe to give Dad a shot. You didn't have throwaway prepackaged syringes in 1946. I was alone in the parlor with Dad.

I didn't know it then, but curiosity has made me an observer, and I automatically started to analyze what was happening. First, I picked up Dad's right arm and noted that it was limp. I looked at his face and noted that his mouth was slightly open but his eyes were closed. Looking at his face, I could not detect if he was breathing. For whatever reason, maybe to understand the whole picture, I started to turn my head to look at his lower legs and feet, but my eyes did not get that far.

In a second, I was aware of something collecting from both his lower body and from his head or upper body at the center of his chest, then rising toward the ceiling. The ceiling was thirteen feet high and the "something" had dissipated just before it reached that point.

None of my physical senses perceived anything, and I felt nothing. The word "whoosh" immediately came to mind to describe what happened.

Now I was back to square one, and my logical mind tried to explain what I had just experienced. I was still holding the arm, and what I had perceived as limp was now really limp! I looked at Dad's face and saw bubbles in his mouth. I know now that they were caused by the last of the air escaping from his lungs, but I didn't know that then. It was over. My two feet took me out of there just as fast as I could go to the kitchen to tell my mother that Dad had gone.

As previously noted, I am a very logical person, and as a result, I tend to observe more closely than some people. A number of events happened in my life that led me to study psychic phenomena. This in turn led me to understand many Bible events and passages that did not make sense if one thought about them. In time, I have learned that one must not only observe the events that register with the five physical senses, but also observe what comes to mind without a physical explanation.

I knew long before I read *The Messengers* that what we call death is only the demise of the machinery that we call a body. It took me a long time, but reincarnation was the only thing that made sense. I understood that the Bible was perhaps more the product of man than of the divine, yet despite the meddling of mankind, it is still the essence of our faith.

So twenty-four years later, when heart disease caught up with Mother, I had a better understanding. Mother had been in a nursing home for only two weeks when she was taken to the hospital. Hospitals now had intensive care units, but not cardiac care units. Because she was a nurse, the nurses in the IC unit knew my mother.

I had to leave the ICU while the nurses tried to stabilize her. About an hour later, they called me in, as her doctor was on the phone. He said that there was nothing more he could do for her. I said I understood and I would stay with her. She had been sedated and could no longer respond to me. I could see the green lines of the EKG and while I didn't understand them, I knew there were supposed to be sharp peaks above and below the center line, not the little hills and valleys that I was seeing.

I sat in an armchair beside the bed. The only light in the room came through the big window from other parts of the IC unit. Because I had a better understanding of what was happening than I did when my father passed, I was not overly upset. I watched the EKG hills and valleys become ever more gentle, and I knew that it would not be long. I had my hands on the arms of the chair and was relaxed when suddenly I felt butterfly wings on the back of my hand closest to the bed. The EKG line was straight. What I felt was not a muscle contraction in the back of my hand or any other physical agent. Again, I use the term "butterfly wings" because that is the description that came into my mind the instant it happened. Mother and I were very close and she had touched me when she left.

Within two months, Mother came to me twice in my dreams, not as a character in a dream but as an intelligent entity. I seldom have meaningful dreams that convey information to me. Many characters I have known, living and not, are part of my dreams. I have had Mother in my dreams many times as a character, but these two times she was spiritually present. She told me that she was all right and happy.

Twice I have been with death and twice I have been vividly aware of the spirit leaving. I am completely comfortable with this knowledge. Perhaps my story will help others to believe, but it will not provide absolute knowledge because they must experience it themselves to know.

Dick Pollins

The Rebirth of Baby Jackie

The angels grew lonely
and called her to play.
Jacqueline Jolaine Pizzagrani
May 22, 1991 – March 3, 1996

That's what's on the headstone of my beautiful baby girl, who shed her shell of flesh and bone and was reborn on March 3, 1996.

I guess this sad tale would have to begin about a month before little Jacula was born. I was coming back from buying some heroin in Vallejo, California, strung out bad and running from a parole warrant.

After I bought my dope, some man I had never seen started disrespecting me, talking to me in a way no man likes to be talked to. I was in a foul mood because I was dope sick, gone too long without my drugs, and upset about a fight my wife and I had had a few days earlier. She had hit me in the head with a shovel and to this day I don't know why. We weren't even having troubles at that point when out of the blue, she whacked me in the head from behind. She was pregnant, so I figured she was mean because of being so uncomfortable. I guess you have to take the good with the bad.

Anyway, I wasn't in a mood to be messed with, especially by someone I didn't know. One thing led to another and I shot the man. I know I reacted that way out of stupidity and foolish pride. I got into a high-speed chase with the police and of course, was caught. One month after, my daughter was born. A few months after her birth, I was sentenced to nine years in prison.

California's half-time law put me back out on the streets after almost five years. During the time I was in prison, my wife was on the run for a few minor charges and was never approved to visit me. My mother came to see me only a few times a year. I didn't get to know my daughter during this time, but we were still close. She knew I was her father and thought I was away at work.

I had a release date of December 25, 1995. In California prisons, if you miss a day of work or lose some time, you lose your parole date. It was important to me to get out on Christmas Day and spend my first Christmas with my daughter. So for almost five years, I didn't miss one day of work and stayed clean so I would have no incident reports. Of course, I was not a model inmate. I used a lot of drugs in prison, not to mention the other stuff. Fortunately, I didn't get caught.

I made my Christmas release date and had a beautiful Christmas in Stockton at my mom's house. Her Christmas present was to have all three of her sons together with her at one time. We've all been in and out of jail since 1978, starting with me at a boys' ranch. The last time my mother had the three of us together was in a youth authority visiting room. I was in one in Stockton and my younger brother was across the street in another. When our mom came to visit, they would bring my younger brother over to my institution. So it had been a while since we had all been around one another.

It was my third Christmas on the streets since 1978. I wanted to make that Christmas parole date in 1995 because at the time I didn't want to wait another year to have Christmas with my daughter. I was sure I'd be doing a parole violation at the very least by that time.

Two months later, I realized the reason I made that Christmas date. It was because it was the only one I'd ever get to spend with my daughter. I guess you could say the angels were looking out for me. I know in my heart they were.

My wife and I were going through some rough times, and she was at her house in Clearlake while I was in the Bay Area, staying on our family boat in the Martinez marina. We got into an argument on the phone and I didn't hear from her for a while after that. When her birthday went by and she didn't call, I knew it was serious and I had to get to Clearlake to work things out or make arrangements for visitation with my daughter.

I didn't have a car and I was trying to get a ride to Clearlake from every person I knew or met who had a car. Clearlake is about a two- or three-hour drive from where I was staying, but for some reason, no one I knew could get me there.

Finally, I got a friend of mine to commit herself to helping me. In return, she wanted me to first straighten out the situation at her house, where wayward dope fiends roosted and were taking advantage of her kindness. I went in and let it be known that I was going to live there now and that the rules of the house had changed. I'm six feet three inches and weigh more than 210 pounds, and am well known for my reputation, so I had no problem running all the street urchins out of her house.

The plan was that after I took care of this business, we were going to drive to Clearlake, spend the night, and come back the next day. The only thing we were waiting on was my friend's check to be delivered by the mail, since it was the first of the month. My friend kept stalling me, and by ten P.M., I finally put my foot down and made her get her stuff together so we could leave. We were on our way!

It was hard traveling because it was night and I didn't know my way there until I got to a certain highway that goes over the mountain in Napa Valley. We finally got to the point where we were supposed to make our way over the mountain, then we stopped at a gas station. I asked a man dumping newspaper bundles off a truck if he knew the way to Clearlake. He pointed straight ahead, so we went that way and eventually went over some mountains and ended up in a town that looked familiar, but wasn't quite what I remembered.

I went into a mini-market and asked where I was. I don't remember the name of the town, but it definitely wasn't Clearlake. The town I was in wasn't even on the map, so that's a lot of miles I missed my turnoff by.

No man wants to admit he's lost, but it wasn't time to be hardheaded, so I asked the clerk how to get to Clearlake. He told me the only way was to go back the same way I'd come until I hit the right junction. Back we went, and after a couple more hours, we ended up right back where we got the wrong directions in the first place. All we would have had to do was take a left turn out of the gas station and an hour and a half later we would have been in Clearlake.

When we finally got there, it was seven in the morning. We had gone four hundred miles out of our way to get there, and after about ten hours on the road, I finally knocked on my wife's door. She opened it and walked away. I came in and gave my daughter a hug and kiss, and after a few minutes, I told my wife that I wanted to go in the bedroom and talk.

After talking for a while, we got everything straightened out, and I decided to stick to my original plan. We were going to spend the night and leave the next day. I wanted to plan my trip so as to run into the guy who was tossing the newspapers at the gas station so I could finish up a little personal business. I was mad at him and intended to let him know just how mad.

My wife and I spent the day around the house and yard with our daughter. We took off to buy her a dollhouse called Polly Pockets, because we had promised it to her a week before. While we were getting it, I looked at the doll next to it and said, "Look at this, baby, it's way tougher than the one we're getting." We got that doll instead.

When we got back to the house and gave the doll to Jackie, she got all excited and hugged me around my legs. "Oh, Daddy! Thank you! This is my favorite doll and I've really been wanting it so bad. Thank you, Daddy. I love you so much." She gave me one of the feelings only a child can give, and I'll never forget it, no matter what happens to me.

We had a beautiful day, and later on, Jackie took her usual evening walk around the block with the old lady next door. When she came back, we were getting ready to have dinner. My sister-in-law and I were drinking some Jose Quervo tequila and having a good time.

I was playing with Jackie when she said, "Daddy, there is a boy around the corner and he had a green sweatshirt on, and it had horses on it. It was ugly and I told him it was ugly, Daddy. The boy hit me right here (she was pointing at her solar plexus) and said he was gonna kill me." Kids say the damndest things, so I said, "He didn't hit you here, did he?" and I pointed to another part of her stomach. I did this a few times and asked her if she wanted to go the hospital.

Why I asked her that, I won't ever know, but she said that she didn't want to go. She had eaten some candy, and a little while later, she said she wasn't feeling good. My wife felt her forehead, which was a little warm, so we put her under the covers and I asked her what she wanted. She said she wanted cold punch and C.J., the dog, and for me to lie down with her.

Early in the morning, my wife and I decided to go out for a drive to iron out our problems. About seven-thirty, I looked in on my daughter and saw that she was uncovered, so I pulled the blanket back over her. She looked at me. I kissed her and said, "Go back to sleep, baby. I'm just covering you up. Daddy's right here." Then I left the house with my wife.

Around eleven, we were driving back down our street when my wife noticed there was an ambulance down the road, in front of her house, in fact. I punched the gas peddle and almost crashed into a cop car as I tried to stop in front of her house. Our world came tumbling down at that moment, and life as we knew it would never be the same for us again.

This is the part of the story that gets sad, but it's a story I feel should be heard so that lessons can be learned, especially for people in jails and prisons who are dealing with the loss of a loved one. It's been over three and a half years since this incident, but I remember it like it was just the other day.

As I stopped the car and got out, the ambulance was leaving. One of the neighbors told us Jackie was in it and it looked like she had black eyes. I ran to my front porch to see what was going on, and there was a cop blocking my front door. I told him to get out of my way, but he told me I couldn't go inside, that our house was a crime scene.

My wife and I and went to the hospital, worried and wondering what was going on. We thought maybe someone had gone inside and robbed my wife's sister and hurt our daughter. When we got to the hospital, a lot of cops were there but no one would tell us anything. They were staying close to us, though.

After an hour, a doctor came out and saw us. We asked what was going on. "Is our daughter okay? Can we see her?" The doctor told us he was going to let us see her, but he wanted to ask us some questions first. That calmed us down. I figured that everything must be all right if he was going to ask us questions. After asking us routine questions, he told us that our daughter didn't make it. I said, "Didn't make what?" Then I saw the look on his face and it dawned on me what he was saying. I said, "You mean she's dead? From what? What happened?" He told us she had died from meningitis.

When we went into the room to see her, a cop was there, and I guess he was waiting to see what our reaction was. There was a woman in our house who had called 911 when she saw Jackie's eyes were black. She told them that someone must have beaten her up and that her parents were gone. Now I understood why the cop said our house was a crime scene. But the doctor said that when you die from meningitis, your whole body will turn the color of a three-day-old bruise, with the thinnest tissues discoloring first.

That's why Jackie's eyes looked black. Since the doctor knew what had caused her death, and it was not abuse, we should have been left alone.

After seeing our daughter, an investigator talked to us and we let him search our house. He wanted to make sure there wasn't anything that would have been lying near our daughter that she might have swallowed. He didn't find anything.

The next day, it came out in the newspaper that there was an investigation into the possible beating death of a four-year-old girl. Over the next two weeks, there were six or seven similar articles. One news station even said that my wife and I were in custody on 187 charges for the beating death of our four-year-old daughter.

Things went very quickly from bad to worse. I don't know why were treated so badly, but it didn't make things any easier while we were trying to hold our family together. We found out there had been an outbreak of meningitis in Clearlake about ten or twelve years prior to this and there had been a few new cases around the time of my daughter's death.

When five people die of a disease around the same time, it has to be declared an "outbreak." Clearlake was a tourist town on its last leg. With tourist season coming up, the locals didn't want to frighten anyone away. So they tried to pass the blame onto us. The original death certificate was altered, and it took seven weeks for an autopsy report to come back.

When my wife got a copy, seventeen pages were missing that the authorities wouldn't give her. For the cause of death, it stated that she died by choking on her own vomit. There was never any report of her vomiting in the ambulance on the way to the hospital, and my sister-in-law was giving her mouth-to-mouth resuscitation until help arrived. As far as we could tell from the autopsy report, they weren't checking to see if she died of any illness, only if she died from ingesting drugs or poison.

We were devastated by the slander and deceit, not to mention from trying to heal ourselves from the death of our beloved daughter.

My wife and I were lying in bed a day or two after Jackie's death, and things were running through my head. I wondered how this was going to affect the rest of our lives, if we would become bitter. All of a sudden, a little poker machine that belonged to my mom started to make noises. It happened about fifteen times during the night. In the morning, I told my mom there was something wrong with her machine because it kept going off all night. "You're lying. The sound on that game doesn't work. Those poker games only play one tune, 'We're in the Money,' when you win," said my mom. But it was making sounds it was not programmed to play.

When my mom said the sound didn't work, my friend messed around with that game for four hours and couldn't get it to make a sound of any kind. That was when I knew it was my daughter messing around with us. I had taught her how to match up the kings, queens, and jacks, and whenever she won she would get excited and yell, "Daddy, Daddy, I won!" Everyone always turned the sound off on that game when they used it, but my daughter would snatch the poker game and turn the sound on to play, and we would always tell her to turn the sound off and quit making all that noise. Of course, she wouldn't.

I know that she was messing with the poker machine that night and I know that she was telling us she was all right and that we should be all right too. I realized that even though this was the worst thing that ever happened to me, I had to always keep faith through all of life's trials. I saw there are blessings during the madness.

I know that it was my angels that didn't let me get a ride to Clearlake until it was the right time to get there. When I was still a day early, I got those messed up directions that caused me to get to Clearlake at seven the next morning. That way, I got to spend my little girl's last day on Earth with her and get that wonderful feeling only a child can give you. If I had not been there when this happened and had not seen how torn up my wife and mother were, I wouldn't have been able to hold it together. I had to be strong for them. But if I had gotten a phone call saying my daughter had died, I would have blown it and probably been killed by the cops in the street somewhere, because I would not have cared.

My family has been blessed with "Jackie sightings." She was a presence with us for about a year since she was reborn in Heaven. After that, she felt we could carry on, so she moved on to whatever new part of her journey she is on.

The point I am making, especially to those in jail, is that no matter how terrible a blow life serves you, including the loss of a loved one, always keep faith and know in your heart you will be reunited with your loved ones again. Our time on Earth is only a brief moment in the life of the cosmos. Our spirits have been around for eternity and the journey does not stop here.

Two months after my daughter died I got locked up and have been in the county jail for the past forty-two months on a serious charge. I probably won't ever see the street again except on a bus ride from one prison to another. My marriage is over and a lot of other hardships have come my way. But the main thing I want to stress is to always keep faith no matter what hardships come your way. Try to recognize your blessings too, no matter how small they might be, and give thanks to our Lord for them. No matter what horrible stuff happens to us, there will be blessings in the midst of it also.

I want to thank The Great Tomorrow for all they've done for me, and Nick Bunick for coming back and sharing the truth with us and answering all the questions we have about religion, the afterlife, and everything else. I also thank you for giving me a chance to share my story with everyone. When some of you out there go through hard times, I hope I can be an example to you that no matter how hard life may get, always keep faith and our Lord and your guides will pull you through. These experiences only bring all of us spiritually closer to God.

Robert Pizzagrani

Babe

I was sixteen years old and had made plans with my boyfriend for the weekend. My mother insisted that my sister and I gather our things to spend the weekend with my grandmother. We lived in Missoula, Montana, but my grandmother lived in Butte and had lost her husband, my grandpa, two years earlier. She was getting ready, with great reluctance, to move to Missoula.

My mother had such urgency in her voice that I dared not argue. We met my grandmother and our cousins early in the day at Georgetown Lake. My grandmother was quite the character, and was her usual Irish self that day. Later we went to the house, and she told me that she did not want to leave the home she had shared so many years with her "Babe," a name she had lovingly called my grandfather.

She told me she wanted to die, and hoped God would be good and take her quickly. I kept saying, "Grandma, come on, you are going to live forever." She selected dishes she wanted me to have and continued to talk about her wish to die.

One night, my mother and grandmother went out to dinner. My cousins, sister, and I slept in the front room.

I heard my mother and grandmother come in about eleven P.M. Then I fell back asleep. An hour later, I heard my grandmother in the bathroom with my mom. She was throwing up, and I rushed in to help my mother hold her up. Within minutes, she slumped over and died. But she was smiling, and to my astonishment, I saw her spirit leave her body.

God was good. I was given a great gift that day, and I have never questioned the existence of an afterlife since then.

Sheila T. Dahsinger

My Beloved

Twelve years ago, my husband and I were married. Two years later, he spent several weeks in intensive care with a liver shunt and barely survived. A year after that, the shunt failed and he was pronounced terminal. After he went through a new experimental operation, it was discovered he had complications from blood clots and was sent home as a hospice patient. Yet he gradually got better. During these times, we shared our faith, strength, and love. Because of my spiritual beliefs, I turned everything over to God, knowing transition is only a door. For this reason, I did not become stressed, but my friends and family could not understand the source of my serenity.

What followed was a loving, learning seven years as my husband gradually became more ill, until he was close to becoming a bedridden invalid. He had promised me he would never become this.

He wanted to last until at least the year 2000, but I sensed a change before the new millennium arrived. We had been putting things in order for quite a while, but now he became more persistent in having me understand the details.

I received in the mail a new set of checks with only my name on them. When I asked my husband why, he said, "I had to order a large amount." One week later, as we were watching a video, he told one last joke to a friend and had a coughing spell that caused a stroke. Seven days later, he quietly slipped away. During those seven days, I played music, shared interesting insights from the book *Experiencing the Soul Before Birth, During Life, After Death* by Eliot Rosen, and told him how much I loved him. He knew he had a wonderful healthy life awaiting him and we would be together again soon.

I used to tease my husband, saying that because he was so protective of me, I knew he would try to become one of my spirit guides. I had wanted some sense of him, for as he was under medication, I could not experience with him the joy in his transition, except by viewing how much younger and more peaceful his face became, especially at the end.

He passed away in the morning, and an extraordinary thing happened later that day. I was sitting at his desk, working on the myriad of details facing me, when his voice message on our phone came on five different times even though no one was calling me. After the fourth time, I chuckled and said, "Yes, I hear you, my beloved. I know you are near."

I have just returned from a wonderful conference on sound healing by Jonathan Goldman with Steve Halpern as a presenter. I asked him if he has considered recording a CD for those who are facing transition and for those who are sharing it with them. I told him that I used his music, especially "Spectrum Suite," when my husband was ill and during his time before transition. He said he was considering it, and I suggested the title "Joyous Transition," because joy means a blessed feeling of peace and happiness in oneness with spirit.

If all couples could live as we did, understanding how precious life is, and make the journey one of awareness, joy, and acceptance, the loved ones remaining would not feel deep grief, but a sense of completion, and have an easier transition to the next part of the journey.

Do I miss my beloved? Oh, yes. Every so often, something will cause me to tear up and then I breathe deeply, releasing in gratitude what we experienced together. Because of the "doingness" I got myself into, I arranged two different retreats during those ten years he was ill, the first in the mountains, the second at the ocean. These retreats were partly to help ease the grief, but mostly to honor the gratitude for the journey. My husband was my teacher, my love, and my friend. No matter how ill he was, he told me and showed me in so many ways how much he loved me, and every day he would tell me how grateful he was to have me in his life. In return, it was my joy, and my service, to create as loving and fulfilling a life for him as he could possibly have.

The other day, I was playing a CD of Chris James, an Australian tenor, in which he sings, "Beloved, you set me free." That is when I realized my beloved, at a soul level, had decided this phase of my journey as well as his was completed, and it was time for us to begin our new travels. Thank you, my beloved. Every day, in every way, I shall do all I can to be worthy of your love.

Sharon Williams

The Music Box

My dad passed away about eleven years ago on November 7. About six weeks later, I was putting up a little artificial Christmas tree that had belonged to him. I was crying and missing him very much.

I went to the other room, and as I stood by the door leading to the hallway, I felt a cold breeze go by me. Still crying, I went back to my room to finish trimming the little tree. There, on one of the branches, was a lock of my dad's hair. I recognized the color, gray mixed with brown. I knew then that he had come to leave me a part of himself. The hair was curled the same way it had been fixed for viewing at his funeral.

The following year on my birthday, he came again. I was touching a music box he had given me, but which had not been played in years. The lid of the box slid off and it played a full tune. I knew it was my birthday present from my dad. It has not played since, although I have tried it many times.

Anna R. Deak

Death's Blessing

The light goes out. The door shuts. Shaking, I dive under the bedcovers. Who will protect me? I worry, afraid death will creep in and snatch me while my parents sleep unaware in the room next to mine. I need a protector, a knight in shining armor. After all, six years old is the age of difficult questions and simple answers.

Stretching eagerly on Sunday morning, I jump out of bed. Cold wooden floors urge my bare feet to move quickly. Socks, shoes, and always a dress—hurrying, I dress to visit God's home. Running down the street, I catch a ride with a neighbor. Saturday evenings occasionally find me at a synagogue, while on any given Sunday, my destination might be a Methodist, Presbyterian, or Catholic church. This is a blessing, for I am left to develop my own relationship with God. My childish mind knows that God is all-loving, everywhere. God—my knight in shining armor, my protector.

The light goes out. The door shuts. As I face the dark, His words are my shield. Hugging my Bible, I snuggle under my blankets and sleep soundly.

Growing up is hard to do. Learning is even harder.

"That's a sin," my friend tells me when she hears I eat steak for dinner on Friday night. "You're going to go to Hell!"

"Rubbish. God loves me. He would never hurt me." But sadly, a part of me listens to her.

The bright sun illuminates the stained glass window,

sending a rainbow of light dancing across the pews. God's love is visible. The preacher says, "God's love is only for a chosen few."

"Do you have what it takes to earn God's love?" he asks from his pulpit. Worrying, I wonder if God still wants to be my knight in shining armor.

"If you don't go to church on Sunday, you're going to Hell," one friend tells me.

"If you're not Catholic, you can't go to Heaven," another says. Crying, I tell the God of my heart that if this is so, we can no longer be one.

Losing my knight is hard, but the preacher's words clearly tell me I am not worthy of God's love. As I place my Bible back on the shelf, loneliness fills my heart. Fearing the silent darkness, I fall asleep by distraction, by TV, radio, or sometimes a book.

Slowly, a cold reality envelops my heart. Knowing I cannot live without verifying what everyone else blindly accepts, I resolve to make one final attempt to know His truth.

"Do You love me? Will You help me and show me the way? I can't do this alone. Please, if You care, tell me the truth."

Continuing to live the life of the young, I wait for an answer but hear nothing. At first. Then the cover of a book catches my eye. Picking it up, I see it is about God, or more correctly, about the life of Saint Paul. I read, and feel my heart lighten with the turning of each page. Remembering my Bible, I pull it off the shelf as a voice within me says, "Listen not to the words of others. Listen to Me and I will tell you the Truth."

Once again, I feel love, but life and death are still a mystery.

Decades pass, and one day the phone rings with the news. My father is dying. Soon we will be separated by a distance I cannot fathom.

"God, I don't understand. Why must he die? Why must any of us die? I'm scared. Help me understand."

Within me, I hear, "My child, you are not the first to ask this question. Many before you have asked and I have answered. The answer to this question is very important, so do not stop until you understand."

Searching, I begin to find the answer. I learn death is not the end but merely a doorway. I learn that we all must talk to God, and He will help us find our own answers. God wants us to ask Him questions so that He may answer each of us directly. There is nothing more meaningful than our relationship with God.

As I come to understand death and its meaning, I come to understand life and its purpose. Death is a blessing, for like any deadline, it forces us to organize ourselves and gives purpose to our actions.

Kendrea Kim Moccia

Some will tell you: reach out and find God, search above and around you and find God. I say to you: look within and find God, for God truly does reside within you.

—In God's Truth

In Memory of Paul

My husband Paul was not outwardly religious or spiritual, but he made a big transition in the last months of his life. I have been on a spiritual journey for the last five or six years. It was most likely for a longer period, but I was not consciously aware of it. During the time I shared my journey with my husband, he would just shake his head and act as if I was becoming a little nuts. However, I sensed that a part of him was still listening and that his male ego was standing in the way.

He was afraid to believe, yet he was afraid not to believe out of concern that he might be left behind. When he was diagnosed with cancer and given only four months to live, things began to change for him. That weekend, I suggested that we do a prayer circle in our home, and it was the first time that he did not give me any static. We had an overwhelming turnout, and I believe from that moment on, my husband started to heal spiritually.

I had been given many signs over the previous two years, and I knew that a physical cure was not in order for Paul. I knew he needed a spiritual healing, so my focus was on that, and if a physical healing happened as well, we would be doubly blessed. Over the four months that Paul was ill, I saw a major transition in him. But what really took me by surprise was the effect that it had on so many others. I didn't fully understand the depth of how we affected people until Paul's funeral. It was such a spiritual experience. Everyone was touched in a special way, including the priest, who delivered an Oscar-performance sermon. It was one like he had never given before, and those who knew him were amazed. I believe that Paul was speaking through him.

I have a thing with the number 11. It started with my finding a dime and a penny. Before the funeral director closed the casket, I put a dime and a penny in the casket and told my husband in a joking way that I wanted to see lots of them, and I told him how special that was to me. The Mass had started and we had a moment of silence, during which I heard coins dropping in the church. My sons looked at me and said, "Mom, did you hear that?"

We knew that one had fallen near us, but we couldn't see it. Shortly after, my son nudged me and said, "Mom look down at your feet." There was a penny. I knew Paul was with us. This has been so great for my boys to witness. They are eighteen and nineteen, and at an age when they don't want to appear foolish; but things kept happening, so that they could not ignore their own spirituality.

At our first prayer circle, we expressed to everyone that we felt Paul's cancer had been a blessing. We felt that if Paul had been killed in a car accident or by a heart attack, it would not have given us the opportunity to say the things we wanted to. Instead, we were given the opportunity for closure, and that was a gift.

During the twenty years I was married to Paul, he was never able to say, "I love you." But in his dying, he learned how, and he gave me that gift. In fact, one day in the hospital, he shocked me and the nurse when out of the blue he said that he was going to live every day that he could, just so he could tell me he loved me. It brings tears to my eyes as I write this, but it also brings me comfort for the healing that took place inside him. I am in awe of how this whole experience strengthened all of us. There has been a birth in death.

Last Mother's Day, I got a rose. I won't go into details but will only explain that even though the flower was dead, the stem began to sprout. I asked the florist if this was a common thing and he said it wasn't. I knew it was a sign, and as I stood there one day looking at this rose, the thought occurred to me that in death there is rebirth. How fitting to receive such a revelation on Mother's Day.

I am now on an incredible journey and realize that I am being directed and will continue to be directed as long as I can keep my ego out of the way.

Ginny Schumacher

Part Four

Dreams

If you are like me, you have had dreams in which a loved one who has passed over appeared to you. In my case, it was my mother and older brother, and occasionally a friend of mine. For me, the dreams are so real that while I am experiencing them, I am not consciously aware that I am dreaming, but believe that I am having an experience with that person.

I am convinced beyond a shadow of a doubt that our loved ones appear to us in our dreams. When we are asleep, we are functioning in a state of mind that is not of the conscious world, but is a combination of our subconscious and the spiritual world. We visit places that we cannot when we are awake, create things we cannot in the daytime, and experience and see things that we cannot while we are awake. I believe our loved ones are able to tap into our dreams while we are asleep, and appear to us while we are in this state of mind.

As you will read in the stories that follow, the person having the dream is being told good-bye by a loved one who had passed. In most cases, the deceased person shares their wisdom and understanding with the person having the dream. And in each case, the person dreaming awakens with a greater understanding of death and a wonderful release of anxiety and pain, because they know there is no such thing as death, only transition, and that their loved one is happy on the Other Side.

Nick Bunick

A Tribute to a Dear Friend

Marie found me. She called me on the phone one day and introduced herself. She said, "I heard you need help finding work. I'll help you. I'll introduce you to some people and you can work with me for a while. If you're as good as I am, I'll give you some of my people."

Those of us who knew Marie knew we had a friend indeed. She and I met and worked together for a time, and she helped me break out on my own. Actually, we helped each other. We laughed, visited each other, went out to dinner, played Scrabble into the wee hours, and remained good friends.

Marie was and is an "angel." You couldn't get out of her house until she gave you something to eat and drink. She worked hard and loved it, and because she did such beautiful work, it was always something to be proud of. She had the patience of a saint! If it didn't come out perfect, she'd start over again until it was the way she wanted it to look. I marveled at her tenacity.

Marie could handle anything. She could always solve problems and give helpful hints when needed. She was a person who took pride in everything, and it showed. She worked side by side with her husband time and again, and Dave took pride in her work also. They were a good team. They knew how to work and how to play. They truly enjoyed life.

There was much love in Marie's heart for everyone and

everything. She called me over to her house one day to see the "scrawny, sick stray cat" that she had fixed a warm bed for. She laughed heartily as she described how it drank the milk nonstop and how the more she fed it, the more it ate. Soon she called to tell me how fat it was getting, and that she hoped now that it was well, it could leave. The next call was, "You'll never guess what happened. We got a bunch of cute little baby kittens. Do you want one?"

For Marie, there was no beating around the bush. She told it the way it was.

In 1994, my father's lingering illness kept me busy and at home. I didn't get to see much of Marie and Dave. In 1995, after my father's passing, I was busy disposing of his properties and tending to his affairs, so again, I would only occasionally run into Marie and Dave.

During this time, I got married and Marie became ill. But that didn't stop her. She continued on, living and enjoying life. She did not want to burden anyone, nor did she want to suffer. She told me she wanted to go quickly and with a smile on her face. I told her I believed in life after life, and she told me she'd have to see it to believe it. We laughed heartily about that. Then I told her that if she found out that I was right, I expected her to come back and tell me about it. She said, "You mean, like haunt you?" I said, "No, Marie. Come and tell me about how beautiful it is there." Marie laughingly retorted, "Yeah, right! Well, I ain't ready yet, so how about if we get together and play some Scrabble?"

The last time I talked to Marie, she asked if she could borrow a dress to wear to her daughter's wedding. She said, "I know you gained some weight since you got married, but so did I, and maybe your dress will fit me." I told her that mine was a bride's dress, not a mother-of-the-bride's dress, and she shouldn't outshine her daughter. She said she would try something else.

I asked when we could get together, and she told me we'd have to wait until they got back from her daughter's wedding. She was so proud of all her children and grandchildren and her family. Her voice getting scratchy, she said we should talk to Dave and make plans for us to go out when they got back. Dave and I talked, and he said he would call me when they got back and we could go to our favorite place, which they had introduced me to years before. We were going to get together in Marie's kitchen—our "favorite place"—and have spaghetti.

Time passed as I waited for the call. I thought that maybe they had decided to stay a while longer and I'd hear from them soon. More time passed, so my husband and I went by their home, only to find that no one was there. I wrote a note and left it on the notepad holder outside the front door. Several times over the next few days, I stopped by the house and even though the door was open, there were no answers to my knocks. I thought they must be visiting someone. I left my business card on the front door, but there was still no response from either Marie or Dave.

One day, I stopped and yelled in the door, "Marie, it's Rene. Is anybody home?" Still no answer. My husband and I made another trip by the house, and the door was still open, but there was no answer. I thought that maybe she was in the shower or taking a nap. We left, talking about the strangeness that there hadn't been any response over the last few days, not even by phone. My husband said, "Maybe she lost her voice again and can't answer." A cold chill swept over me as I pondered his words.

Time marched on. One Monday evening, some friends came over and we were meditating. I had forgotten to turn off the phone, and it began to ring. My urge to answer it was very strong. My husband and I both went into the kitchen and he picked up the phone. It was Rose. "Tell Rene our best friend, Marie, died."

I took the phone in disbelief. "Rose, what happened?" Rose could hardly speak. She told me it happened Friday and that Dave was in Pennsylvania at their daughter's house. I took down the number and told Rose I'd get back to her later. I asked the prayer group to pray for my dear friend,

Marie. It became silent as the prayers were mentally sent out. During the prayer, I asked Marie to come and talk to me. When I felt her presence, I asked, "Marie, what happened?" The thought of cancer crossed my mind. She answered, "It happened so fast that I didn't even know myself, but it wasn't from what you think. Call Dave. He'll tell you all about it. Call Dave." I almost cried, wondering what could have happened. Marie spoke to me again, "It wasn't the cancer. It was my heart. Call Dave."

The next day when I got Dave on the line, I asked him what happened. He told me that it shouldn't have happened. He told me it was heart surgery that had failed. We talked for a while and he said he'd be back in town in a few days. He had to go because of other calls he was receiving, so I told him to take care of himself and that we would talk when he got home.

A few days later, at approximately six A.M., I was awakened by the feeling of a presence over my bed. I jumped out of bed, and as I crossed the room, the presence grew stronger. As I returned to bed, I felt I was about to receive a message. My eyes felt heavy and as I closed them, I saw a newly constructed double house, like a duplex. The two homes were not side-by-side, but front-to-back connected by a hallway. I saw myself looking over this new construction and walking into a bathroom in the front one. The bathroom had no walls, but it did have a brand-new bathtub. There was a white facecloth on the sink and a bar of soap. I picked up the cloth with the intention of washing my face and realized there was no water available. Behind the tub was a crawl space under the floor. I walked back into the hall, where I could see the second half of this new structure, and saw a living room newly furnished, and a bedroom farther back.

A married couple was sleeping in the bedroom. I realized I was in someone else's home, so I went back to the bathroom. Suddenly, the couple came in there also. The woman was wearing a white turtleneck, long-sleeved shirt, and light-colored blue jeans. The man was wearing dark trousers and no shirt. He came in the room second and saw that there was no water in the bathroom. He asked his wife to get him a tool. She brought it to him and he reached beside the tub and cut a pipe. He gave it to me, saying, "Be sure to ask the master plumber to fix my plumbing for me." I agreed to do this. His wife then said, "There is someone here to see you."

She pointed to the hallway. I walked over to Marie, who was standing there with a little girl about three or four years of age. They were both beautifully radiant. Marie and I wrapped our arms around each other and cried with joy. "Oh Marie, you look so beautiful!" I cried. I laid my head on her shoulder and we cried together. Then I realized my tears were getting her long gown wet on the shoulder. I apologized, and we looked lovingly into each other's eyes. "You look so beautiful. Where are you going?" I asked her. "To a wedding," she replied. The little girl was also wearing a long gown. Both gowns were plain but elegant, and Marie and the girl each wore a ring of flowers around her head.

One wore a pink gown and the other yellow, but I can't remember who wore which color. I wore a gown of the same type. The child never spoke, but stayed constantly at Marie's side. It was obvious there was much love between them. Every step Marie took, the child was at her side. We talked about love and forgiveness, and other things, including how happy we were to see each other. Then she told me they had to go, and she asked me to walk outside with them. We crossed a street and stood at an intersection, talking and embracing once more. I told her to remember when she got to the wedding to ask everyone for their forgiveness for anything and everything and to tell them that she also forgives them for anything and everything that ever happened. But I told her most of all to show them love. "Tell them how much you love them," I said. "I will," Marie answered.

Suddenly, a long, black, shiny Cadillac limousine pulled up to the sidewalk and Marie and I embraced once more and said good-bye. The child got in first and Marie followed. As the limousine pulled away, I awoke with a start, but with a very happy heart.

I write this with much love and respect for my dear and wonderful friend, Marie. In my heart I know that she is at peace and is radiating love to all those who were in her life. The memory of this dream-vision will never fade. It is imprinted indelibly in my memory. I'll see you in my dreams again, Marie.

Lourene Jurkovic

Before you came to this Earth plane, you existed in the spirit dimension. You were, and are, a child of God. God created you from God's spirit. Your relationship to God is that of a tree to a forest, as a drop of water is to a lake, a grain of sand is to a beach. You are a part of the whole. You are a part of the Creator. You are part of the divinity. You are part of God.

—In God's Truth

My Dream Visit to the Next Life

Before my grandfather Harry Lee died, he and I made a pact in which he promised to contact me after death if he could find a way of doing so. Because we weren't entirely serious, I soon forgot about this. I certainly wasn't thinking about it when Pa—I always called my grandfather "Pa"—became seriously ill in the spring of 1967.

When I talked with Pa one day on the phone, he assured me he was all right and did not need a doctor. That was Pa's way. He complained little and would go to a doctor only when we insisted. But little more than a week after our conversation, he had a stroke and died.

One night shortly before his passing, I had a beautiful and inspiring dream. In this dream, Pa revealed to me the amazing details of his transition to the next life. It was as if I had been allowed to visit the next life with Pa and to observe what happened to him there. After his death, I missed him terribly, but the memory of that dream, which I saw as Pa's way of fulfilling our pact, comforted me immeasurably during those difficult days.

Perhaps our closeness had made such contact possible. Pa and I had been buddies from my childhood. Although he was sixty-four when I was born, I never thought of him as an old man, nor did he think of himself as one. He was always active on the forty-five-acre vegetable farm that my parents and grandparents worked together in the Kansas River Valley near Kansas City.

I was an only child growing up in a secluded area with four adults, but I didn't miss children my own age, because Pa and I behaved like a couple of youngsters. Pa saw life as a grand adventure and he made it that way for me as well. Whether we were romping through the fields, fishing in the farm pond, or sitting on the front porch of the old farmhouse on a summer evening, the time I spent with Pa was exciting. Sometimes Pa would tell stories of his childhood, or of his travels through the United States and Mexico as a bridge construction foreman. Somehow, no matter how many times he told a story, he always managed to make it interesting.

I marveled at Pa's patience and tolerance. He seldom got angry, but when he did, he practically never swore. To him, "shucks" was a strong word. He was kind to people and animals alike. He was polite, honest, and generous, and he regarded nearly everyone as a friend. In short, he was a very special man.

Pa was psychic, although I doubt that he ever knew the meaning of the word. He loved his wife Alice through more than fifty years of marriage and continued to love her after she died. He told me his wife had appeared to him twice after her death. He said there was a light above her and that it lit up the room as they talked.

Pa also saw my mother, Thelma, walking around the house after she died near my father, Cecil Lee. He did not recognize her at first, because she looked so young. I later learned that after death, people frequently come through psychically as young—around college age.

Just three months before Pa's death, he told me he had dreamed he had three years to live. That would have made him one hundred years old. But it turned out to be three months, not three years.

Two days after talking with Pa on the telephone for the last time, I came down with the mumps. I was confined to bed for eleven days, the longest illness I have ever had.

On the night I dreamed about Pa's transition, I was especially ill. I had no way of knowing that Pa had suffered his stroke that night, because my wife Dorothy thought it best not to tell me about it until I felt better. The next morning, I had recovered sufficiently to record my dream in a notebook. As I was writing, I told my wife I had had a wonderful dream.

As I related it to her, we both realized it was about my grandfather's transition. She said Pa was in the hospital, where he had lingered a week, hardly recognizing those who came to visit. He told Dorothy that he had seen my deceased mother and grandmother standing by his bedside.

Although I could not be with him physically, it seemed to me that in my dream, Pa and I had been together spiritually. Some people might say mine was a clairvoyant vision, but I felt I had had an out-of-body experience. Pa showed me what his new life would be like a week before his actual physical death.

When the dream began, I found myself in the company of a young man dressed in a brown suit. Later, I realized that this was how Pa had looked seventy or eighty years before. We ascended through a blue mist until we came to a huge, beautiful campus in the sky, or in some other dimension. I sensed that darkness never fell on this campus, that it was always bathed in light.

We walked across spacious, tree-lined lawns to a gigantic

dome-shaped auditorium, which we entered through a side door. I was startled to see millions of people seated about this huge amphitheater. There were so many seats, they appeared to stretch to infinity. Other people came through the same door we had entered, and still others came in through different entrances. Somehow, I felt that most of these people had come from Earth before we did.

I was more concerned, however, with what each person was doing. Pa sat down in one of the chairs and was given a huge book, which I thought was the Bible. Everyone except me had such a book. Although I did not have it with me, I was sure I had one somewhere. Because I didn't want to miss anything, I chose to stay exactly where I was and to be content to read over my companion's shoulder.

Although the young man who was Pa said nothing, we seemed to communicate telepathically. I felt the guidance and presence of an all-knowing spiritual force that all of us shared. I saw no God-figure, only strong, beautiful adults. There were no old people and no children.

Each person had the task of reading one paragraph from the huge book. The lettering came off the page not only to meet the eyes but to engage the other senses as well. It was as if the thoughts entered my being.

Each paragraph explained a way in which consciousness could be expanded. Some of the lessons were acted out on a bright brown stage in the center of the auditorium. The first action lesson showed how mental telepathy works, and from it, I came to understand that each person in the auditorium was psychically linked with all the others. They knew each other truthfully and totally, and all of them wanted it that way.

One person read a passage about strawberry jam, and every person, including me, could "taste" the jam in his mind. Another read about how a bird feels when it is singing. All of us felt the joy of a whistling bird.

Someone else played a piano on the stage, and I felt the notes and saw beautifully colored chords welling up from the instrument. When one person thought of a beautiful landscape, I felt as if I were in the landscape also, sniffing the scented breeze and experiencing a great peace.

I felt I could consider a complicated mathematical problem and find the answer without going through the normal step-by-step procedures. I was aware somehow that all knowledge was available here, even the power of creation. I saw a person think intently of a sweet potato until one materialized in his hand.

A man went to the stage to illustrate greed and lust. Suddenly, he disappeared. I wondered what had happened to him but then sensed he had gone back to the Earth to be born again and to live another life. Perhaps in this new life, he would learn to control his greed and lust.

I wondered what happened to those people who remained here. Maybe this was like a college orientation session. These people all had lived on Earth and now had come back for further education before returning to the world once more. This seemed to be the real life, whereas life on Earth was like a two-week laboratory experiment in which a few personality or character traits were tested and shaped.

Pa met a young lady with long beautiful black hair. I did not know her initially. Later, after looking at photographs of my grandmother as a young woman, I realized she was the young lady and that the love my grandparents had for each other on Earth continued here, and if anything, seemed greater.

A crowd of people came up to greet my grandfather. I assumed they were friends and relatives but I didn't recognize any of them. They were very happy to see him, and I could feel their joy at this reunion.

At that point, Pa let me know that without a book, I could not stay on the campus any longer. As the dream began to fade, my consciousness gradually drifted back to my body where it lay asleep with the mumps. But ill as I was when I awakened, tears of joy were streaming from my eyes.

I recovered from the mumps in time to attend Pa's funeral. Only a few people were there, because Pa was so old that most of his friends had died long before.

At the funeral, Pa gave my father and me a message. He made it clear that he wanted no one to be sad about his passing. My father, who had cried over Pa's grave, heard a voice that seemed to ring through the countryside so loudly that everyone should have heard it, but only Dad was aware of it. The voice told him to be gone from the grave and to cease his sorrow.

My own final contact with Pa had taken place just before that, as we followed the hearse to the cemetery. I heard the chorus of "Onward, Christian Soldiers" being played over and over on an organ. It did not occur to me at first that the others could not hear it. In fact, I asked the driver if he had music playing on a car tape. He gave me a strange look and said no.

While the song was inaudible to everyone else, I heard it distinctly. I recognized it as a psychic message from Pa, who was doing more than just saying good-bye; he was encouraging me to go on with my life, just as he was going on with his.

If all goes well, I am sure that someday Pa will help me find my book in my locker on that campus from my dream, and that he and I will be permanent companions in life's greatest adventure.

Herb Lee

Love Everlasting

It was crunch time. I was rushing out the door to catch a plane to Texas. It was the first time in a couple of years that my whole family would be together. My siblings and I were spread out over three states, and it was difficult coordinating our visits.

As I was grabbing my suitcase, the phone rang. I did not have time to answer but could not resist the temptation to do so. It was my mother, crying on the other end. My dad had just had a massive heart attack. I could tell by her voice that he did not make it. "Mom, just wait for me," I screamed into the receiver. "I will be right there!"

On the plane to Texas, I sobbed over the fact that I had missed being able to tell my father I loved him before he left us.

By the time I arrived at my mother's house, she was surrounded by my three brothers comforting her and taking care of all the necessary arrangements. We were grateful to be able to be at her side in this special time of need. How ironic that Dad would pass on just as the family was coming together.

That night, I woke up, startled by a vivid dream. Actually, it was more like a vision or a video playing in my head. It was of my father on the front porch of his shop. That is where he had his heart attack and had died. He was on his knees looking up into the heavens, surrounded by a white light. He was saying, "Thank you, God."

Admittedly, I have never been too interested in my dreams. Usually I do not remember them, or if I do, they are too confusing to make sense of. I knew this one was different. It was my dad telling me that this was the way he wanted it. When I related this to my mom and brothers, we all had to agree. It had been perfect. Dad was not sick. (He was never a good patient.) He had just finished riding his bicycle to the fix-it shop to start his day. If he had been asked—and perhaps he was asked—my father would have chosen this transition, including the time, location, and the way it happened.

As people came to visit, stories would unfold of how loved ones had just received a letter from Dad. My twin sons, who were in Spain at the time, received their letter several days after his funeral. They, along with others, marveled at his beautifully written words of pride and encouragement. Friends and family would now always have a memento of love from this very special man. Other acquaintances told us of how he had relinquished different duties to them over the past couple of months. It seemed to everyone that his "sudden" death had actually been anticipated.

When we buried his body, almost five years ago, we experienced his undying love. It was a palpable feeling all of us noticed. Now when I talk to family, we frequently mention happenings that affirm Dad's presence with us. An example is when I was going through my photographs and discovered one of Dad with a big grin, standing next to his bicycle at the very place he had passed on.

Since the passing of my father, I will never look at death in the same way. I will be more aware of signs from my loved ones on the Other Side, which I think help erase the sense of loss. More important, I have learned that love never dies. It seems to grow and become more intimate. I have found new meaning in the term "love everlasting."

Candace Borja

God is not multi-dimensional. God is exclusively, unequiv-ocally not a duality, but a manifestation of love. Can one who knows only love be capable of punishing? Can one who generates only love cause heartache or hardship? God can only manifest love, for God is love.

—In God's Truth

Mother, I Love You

I am writing this letter from prison. Back in July of 1994, my mother came to visit me, along with a friend who was also coming to visit her son. My mother was very ill at that time, but she still loved me enough to come for a visit. She was having heart problems and had asthma. She was, in fact, waiting for a heart transplant and was on various medications to help her cope. Even with all that, she still wouldn't stop smoking. The visit with her went great that day, and I was very happy to be with her.

About two days following that visit, I was told that my mother had died at her sister's house. Her heart had stopped. I was in pain. I loved her deeply and felt it was my fault she died because of the lack of love I had shown her. I felt that I had deeply hurt her by having gone to prison.

I called my friend's mother, who had brought her to see

me on that last visit, and I told her the sad news. She told me what my mother had said as they were leaving the prison that day. My mother told her that she didn't want to die until I got out of prison. But she died only two days later. Fortunately, they allowed me to go to the church service for her funeral.

That night I cried. I cried for not having told her that I loved her, and I was sorry for many things I had done before she died. Inside myself, I basically prayed to say good-bye and to say, "I love you," to my mother.

My mother came to me that night in my dream. We were talking on a bus, though I am not sure what we were talking about. Then the bus stopped, and as I was getting off, I turned around to my mother, but she stayed seated. She said to me, "Good-bye, son, I must go on now. I love you."

I know she went on into the spirit world, for that was the last time I have seen her. I know she went home, and the pain within me has stopped. This story is written in memory of my mother, Donna Flippo—and yes, Mother, I love you.

Joseph Flippo

Healing Dreams

Katie woke up after one hour of sleeping on a Wednesday night with a bad headache. She said, "Ouch," snored, and then had a seizure. She went to the hospital and immediately underwent emergency brain surgery, but it was too late. She never woke up from her coma. I made the decision to allow her to be an organ donor. After about fifty hours of no sleep and praying the rosary at her side in the hospital, I was finally able to sleep for more than five minutes. When I did, I had the most vivid dream

I went to bed exhausted, and was considering not telling Katie's best friends from New Jersey about her death. I thought it was better they think she was rude or that maybe she had lost her address book. I admit, this was a cowardly fantasy, but it would have broken my heart all over again to have to tell her fourth-grade friends about her passing.

In my dream, Katie and I were in my car driving the interstate through the Texas panhandle, just as we had in real life weeks before. Suddenly, an eighteen-wheeler crashed into the passenger-side door, instantly killing Katie. I rushed to her and pulled her body from the wreckage. I was devastated. Then over my left shoulder I heard Katie's voice. I turned, and there she was, perfectly whole and healthy!

"Oh, Mom! You are not paying attention. I am not there anymore. That is just my body. Gee, Mom, you are so caught up in hugging my body that you did not notice that the truck that hit us is a New York City cheesecake truck.

Now listen carefully. I want you to take enough cheesecake off the truck before it spoils so that you can give a piece of cheesecake to everyone I love. I may not have a body but I can still love. And since you do have a body, you must call and write to all the people I love and you must tell them that my body is gone. I cannot write to them anymore, but I still love them. Don't let anyone believe I have forgotten them. In fact, I would like you to give a piece of this very delicious cheesecake to each and every person I love, and as they are eating it, please tell them that I love them as much as that cheesecake is delicious."

I was still in shock in my dream, and I hesitated. Katie started loading my car up with cheesecake, and beautiful gilded wrapping paper appeared out of thin air. Katie was wrapping large triangles of cheesecake, telling me, "This one is for Maryann, this is for Alyssa, this is for Laura. . . ."

I awoke from the dream having no cowardly thoughts, but rather, a sense of peace. I was able to tell all of Katie's friends about her passing. We flew back to New Jersey for her funeral, and everyone came: her nursery school teachers, summer camp counselors, grade school teachers and principals. Every babysitter she ever had, her classmates and friends, our chiropractor, neighbors, the real estate guy that sold our New Jersey house— these came too. Everyone she ever loved on Earth came. We had about 750 people at her funeral on a weeknight in northern New Jersey, where most people are consumed by the rat race of commuting to their jobs in New York City.

A few weeks later, I had another fear addressed by a dream. I felt I should have known ahead of time of Katie's illness so that I could have warned or protected her. I work with a very gifted hands-on healer who believes in Christ, and I have witnessed miracles around that healing work. I thought, "How could I have missed this? I should have done something to protect her. Maybe if I had known, I could have found the way to heal the aneurysm. Katie had so much love for Jesus, so much zest for life. I know she was destined to do great things on Earth!"

I had another vivid, wake-up-in-a-cold-sweat dream. Somehow, the angels heard my concerns and took pity on me. I was taken to a room that felt like a court in Heaven. I heard and felt (but did not see) angels. They asked me, "Would you like to go back in time and relive this episode?"

"Oh, yes! Thank you." I was given the chance to go back two weeks in time before my daughter's aneurysm. In the first part of the dream, I decided I should tell Katie what would happen and see if maybe we could act on her last wishes. I tried to tell her, but her beautiful happy face and sparkling eyes broke my heart. I did not have the courage. A week went by, and I realized I must tell her, but she had already died a week ahead of schedule. I was immediately brought back to angel court. They asked me, "Was that what you wanted?"

I cried out, "Noooooo! Please give me another chance. I was too chicken. Please let me do it over."

Thankfully, they let me do it over.

This time I purposefully decided to not tell her. I decided to pour every ounce of mother's love into her. I gave her my all. I used everything I had learned from doing healing work, and amazingly, Katie did not die in two weeks. She lived on, and I felt years passing, like an epic film. I saw highlights from each year. Katie and I shared much joy, and she matured into a poised and lively young woman of seventeen. She went to her prom. I saw myself taking photos of her in her prom gown. She came home hours later and went to sleep and died of the aneurysm that night. As I discovered her dead body, I was whisked back to the angel court. They asked me again, "Was that what you wanted?"

I exclaimed, "Well, of course. I had seven more magnificent years with Katie. I thoroughly enjoyed every moment. We shared much love and joy."

Then the angels allowed me to see them, and they looked very sad. "Oh, Maryann, this is tragic." They handed me a mirror. "Look at yourself," they commanded.

When I saw myself in the mirror, I was wrinkled and had aged fifty years. I was tired and gray and pale and worn-out.

The angel council explained, "To do this drained you, because from Heaven's point of view, Katie's soul was ripe at age ten. It did not hurt her soul to remain here for the extra seven years, but she had no juice from Heaven left for her Earth life because Heaven was ready for her. So you had to use your own energies to keep her here. That is why you aged at an accelerated rate. Now the tragedy is that you are too tired to live out the destiny your soul had hoped this life would meet." The angels shook their heads in sadness and pity.

I awoke this time feeling that maybe my arms were too short to box with God. Maybe the best way it could be was the way it was. I love you, Katie. Thank you for your love and life during the short time you were with me.

Maryann DeStefano

My Bradley

It was over ten years ago, yet I still remember that night as if it were yesterday. It was a warm May evening in 1988. The stars were out, twinkling and bright. I was standing outside in the darkness looking at the night sky. I was praying, crying, talking to God. I was angry, grieving, and depressed. My brother Bradley had died of cancer at twenty-nine two weeks before that very night, and I missed him very much.

He had been more than a brother, for Brad was always there when I needed him. I depended on him for so much. My life was difficult, as I was married to an alcoholic and trying to raise two young sons. But Bradley was always giving me support. He was always someone I could talk to. I could tell him anything, and he would simply nod his head knowingly, never critical or judgmental.

Brad had lived with my husband, my sons, and me on and off for ten years. He had fought the battle of cancer for eight of those last years. Six months before he died, he had moved back into our home and was getting weaker and thinner, but I was in denial and could not see it.

One day during this period, a neighbor said that Brad had come home to die. It was as if the neighbor had slapped me across the face. I could not accept it.

The last day of Brad's life came suddenly, and it was a shock. We had been sitting around the kitchen table eating supper, laughing and joking. Brad got up to leave. He was going out to see his girlfriend and then go to work.

He worked as a sound man for a local band. Even though he was weak and coughed most of the time, he loved being part of the band and would not give it up. His coughing became so bad that he would have to wear a surgical mask and have an air purifier sitting on the sound mixer when he worked in smoke-filled clubs.

But that night, he did not make it to work. Thirty minutes after he left the house, I got a call to go to the emergency room. Brad had gone into respiratory arrest. My oldest son Patrick went with me to the hospital. My husband stayed home with Tony, our youngest. At the hospital, the doctor told me Brad was dying. The cancer had taken over his only lung and there was nothing they could do. The doctor gave me a choice of putting him on a ventilator or just letting him go in peace. I screamed to myself, "No, not me. I can't decide!"

I was allowed to see him. Brad had tubes in his nose and mouth, and his hands were tied to the rails of the stretcher. I untied him, and he grabbed my hands. Holding my hands tightly in his, he looked steadily into my eyes, and it came into my mind just as clearly as if he had spoken: "You know what this means?" I nodded my head, "Yes." The nurse just stared at us through this silent exchange. I made the decision to let him go. He was moved to a hospital room and died three hours later.

I had gone to the hospital with Patrick, and when Brad was moved to his hospital room, I called my family to join us. My father, my other brother, my husband, and our boys were at Brad's side when he died. Even after he stopped breathing, his heart—that magnificent heart—continued beating for a while.

The funeral went by in a blur. Each day following it, I became more depressed, until two weeks to the day after Brad's death. On that particular night, my husband had come home from work and declared that life was too short, he hated his job, and had quit it.

"Oh, no," I thought, "How can I go to school now?" I

had planned to start nursing school that fall. Now with my husband quitting yet another job, I did not see how that could happen. I would have to keep my job. For five years, I had planned and waited to get into nursing school; now it was gone! Everything was gone. Bradley was gone. Life seemed too hard. The struggle to just live seemed too difficult.

So I went out into the yard that night to be by myself, and I started to cry and pray. I asked God why life was so hard, and for what? To struggle and live in pain, only to die like Bradley? And what about Bradley? Where was he? Was he in Heaven or Hell? Was there a Heaven and a Hell? Was there really life after death? Dear God, give me a sign, let me know he is alive, that his soul lives on somewhere.

Then I thought, "No, things like that do not happen." My mother died of cancer when I was twelve years old, and there was never a sign. There was nothing. I felt then that I did not want to struggle anymore. I just wanted to die too.

My husband, a Vietnam veteran, had a large bottle of tranquilizers sitting on top of the refrigerator. He took the pills for his "nerves." If I could take enough of them, I could end it all. But I was too tired and depressed to take them that night. Without thinking of my children or family, I decided that if I still felt the same way the next morning, I would kill myself.

I went inside past my husband, who was watching television on the couch, and went to bed. Instead of saying my nightly prayers, I simply stated, "I don't give a damn if there is a Heaven or a Hell, I want to cease to exist," and went to sleep.

I fell asleep right away and started to dream. In my dream, someone was calling to me out of a gray swirl. When I recognized it was Bradley, he became clear to me. I hugged and kissed him. It was so joyous to see him. I could not believe it. It was him. It was really him. I asked excitedly, "Brad, what are you doing here?"

Brad stated, "This is what you asked for out in the yard." I was shocked. Did someone hear my prayers? This was the strangest dream. I could see my body was still in my bed, but Brad and I were standing in his room.

I asked him if our prayers and our love for him helped, and he said, "Yes." I asked, "Is it nice where you are?" He said, "Yes. Someday you will know how nice it is." I understood him to mean not now, that it was not my time. He said that he was fine and did not know why I was so upset. As considerate as he had been in life, he asked, "Is there anything that you need?" I replied, "Just your love." Then he was gone, and I was sitting up in bed in awe of what had just happened. I felt a great peace and knew then that I would never again consider taking my life. I got down on my knees and thanked God for hearing my prayer, for sending Brad to save my life. In great humility, I asked for forgiveness for temporarily losing my faith.

There have been many struggles since that night, but I know I am never alone in them. I draw great strength knowing that our heavenly Father is always there and hears our prayers, even out in the darkness of the night or during great despair. Peace be with you.

Constance Viar

Master Antonio

I was half-awake and half-asleep, but I was aware of two words printed in capital letters above my upper visual screen: "Texaco Chief." I pondered the meaning of the words and reminisced. The only Texaco person I knew was my dad, but he wasn't a chief. He just had worked there for twenty-five years until his retirement. Slipping back into a deep sleep, I could see myself in an old house on a hill. I took a long wooden-handled tool, similar to a rake, and began to clean my yard of debris.

A large, round piece of junk came loose and rolled down the hill towards my neighbors' house. The Galligans lived across the street from me in my hometown of Joliet, Illinois. I wondered what they'd say when they discovered it. "Oh well, it's their junk anyway," I thought.

I could hear the telephone ringing inside my house, so I ran into the kitchen and picked it up. It was an old wooden wall phone. "Hello?" I said.

My dad responded, "Hi, Rene, how are you?"

"Just fine," I answered. "A little tired but just fine."

"That's good," said Dad.

"Dad, is that you?" The connection was a bit distorted at times and I had to make some adjustments.

"Yeah. I'm just checking up on you and I want to tell you that I'm moving into a small apartment. I'm not in my house anymore," Dad said in his matter-of-fact way.

I walked around a little, pulling the telephone cord with

me. "I can't hear you very clearly, Dad. Let me make some adjustments to my radio. It must be off the station." I could hear a buzzing noise like static.

"Okay," Dad responded patiently.

I tuned the radio to the proper frequency band and turned the music down as I walked into an empty room in my house. I noticed the room had old wooden floors. Looking up at the large picture window, I saw a woman walking by. She looked up at me but kept walking. She was wearing light-colored clothing, slacks and a blouse with short sleeves. A tall, rather thin woman.

"Dad, can you hear me?" I asked.

"Yeah. That's better," he replied.

"Where did you say you moved to?"

"A small apartment. I put some money down on it and . . ." (I couldn't hear him again because of the static. He said he either bought it or rented it, I'm not sure.)

"I can't hear you, Dad. Let me shut my radio off and turn up the hearing aid volume on the telephone." (I adjusted my hearing aids.) "Now, say that again?"

"Remember Mr. . . ." (I lost the recall of this name as I later wrote this vision down.) "I moved into his apartment. I feel much better here."

"Oh, well, I am glad to hear that. What's all that crying and carrying on in the background, Dad?" (There was a woman wailing, screaming, and crying out.)

"It's Julie, honey. She's going to die and she's very frightened. I want you to go to her. She needs you."

"Okay, Dad. I will."

"It's important, honey. She can't handle it."

I heard Julie's cries and laments in the background behind Dad. Suddenly, I felt lots of electrical impulses in the back and top of my head, resonating in two vertical columns of energy, and I realized that I was talking to my dad in a strange setting. Now I was fully awake and aware.

"Dad, am I really talking to you? Is this really you, Dad?" I was now realizing that my father was "dead." He passed over on November 30, 1994, at eighty-eight years of age.

His words came very clearly and very precisely. "It's me, honey, and yes, you are really talking to me and I'm really talking to you. Now, don't forget about my friend, Julie."

My emotions began to well up inside of me, and I felt like a bubble ready to burst. I wanted to be sure. "Dad, you died almost a year ago, how can you be calling me on the telephone? Is this really you, Dad?"

"Yeah, honey, you know it is! I've got to go now. I love you. Remember Julie," he repeated.

"It's really you, Dad! I love you!" I sobbed. I sobbed with love and joy and ecstasy. I got out of bed and searched for a paper and pencil to record this amazing telepathic dream-vision connection with the "Texaco Chief," my father, Master Antonio.

Being so moved by this miraculous event, I looked through my dad's old notes and business cards until I found Julie's name and number. I called her and told her that my father had come to me in a dream-vision and asked me to see her. I did not give her the details, only that Dad wanted us to meet each other. How happy she was to hear from me, so much so that she insisted that my husband and I come to visit right away. She gave us the directions, and we left within an hour and a half. Inwardly, I felt that something special was going to be made known to me. I mentioned this to my husband and told him I thought she might be the woman in my dream-vision.

Upon our arrival, I said a prayer in my mind and asked Dad to be with us in spirit. The door opened, and I stood there speechless. I was looking at the woman who had walked past the window in my dream-vision. It was her! My husband and I looked at each other knowingly.

After much hugging and all of us trying to talk at once, we settled into a tour of the house and conversation about her old times with my dad, as they had known each other for twenty-five years. They had been dance partners, and

Julie told me that she had met me at a dance eleven years earlier. I remembered being there with Dad, but he had introduced me to so many people that I didn't remember Julie. My husband and I took her to lunch and talked and laughed endlessly. She was so much fun.

When we returned to her house, Julie presented me with a beautifully wrapped wedding present of kitchen linens. They were a perfect match for our kitchen; the wrappings were of white doves and pink and dusty-rose-colored roses, which were our wedding colors and decor. It was very touching. She had had no idea of my wedding theme.

As we hugged each other, Julie said that she could feel my dad's presence in the house and that he was very pleased we had gotten together. We reminisced about Dad's illness, and she told us that she would not ever want to go through anything like that. We promised prayers for each other and parted, knowing that we would remain good friends and call each other from time to time, as well as get together occasionally for lunch.

A few months passed with an occasional letter, card, or call to each other. The 1995 holidays were busy, and bouts with influenza kept everyone at home. Time seemed to get away, and we did not connect for a while. I wondered if Dad had been wrong about Julie. Then a message on my answering machine left me worried. Julie wanted to hear from us. She sounded very weak. When I returned her call, she told us she had gone to a doctor to have a small lump on her upper chest examined. She had been admitted into the hospital and had it removed immediately, just to be on the safe side. She was awaiting the results, and assured us that it was not cancer. We offered her our prayers. She was grateful and asked us to continue them.

Again, I wondered about my dad's visit to me in the vision. Dad's words came back to me: "Julie is going to die and she can't handle it. I want you to go to her. She needs you." I tried to erase the words from my mind, but they remained and would surface from time to time.

On Friday, January 11, we came home to find another message on the answering machine. Julie's voice was almost hysterical. She was going back for another operation. The doctor finally had given her the news that she had cancer and it was spreading. When I returned her call, we talked about life and death. Her attitude had changed to a more positive one. She asked us to continue our prayers for her, and we guaranteed this.

Following the surgery, Julie said the cancer had spread and that she had a caretaker at home now. She wanted all the morphine she could get to ease the pain, because she couldn't handle it. She just wanted to go to sleep and not wake up. She wanted no visitors because she said she did not look like herself. I assured her that I was not interested in how she looked, for I knew the beauty in her heart. She agreed that once she was moved into a care facility, I could come and visit her. She told me to come on June 14, when she would be settled in.

Time slipped away. Suddenly, I realized it was past June 14. How could I have forgotten? Frantically, I looked for the new telephone number she had given me. A voice on the other end asked if I was related to Julie. I said I was not, but that she and my dad had been friends for twenty-five years and we had become friends through my dad. I was asked to wait. For some reason, I thought the next voice I heard would be Julie's.

Suddenly a voice came on the line. "I am the supervisor. Julie never made it here. She did not get to move in. She died on June 14."

Slowly, as the words penetrated, I thanked her and hung up. Dad's words came back to me. I prayed for Julie.

There was no memorial service. The telephone was disconnected, Julie's house had been sold, and there was no way of contacting anyone. I often wondered what happened to Julie's family. I remembered her saying she had not been in touch with them for years. I drifted off to sleep one night, pondering these thoughts. A sudden movement of my bed startled me awake. Seeing nothing, I closed my eyes and found myself again in a dream-vision. I was in a quaint little house, standing in a small room that was rolling backwards downhill along a winding sandy pathway with flowers on both sides. Suddenly, the little house stopped rolling and the front door opened. There was a beautiful field of yellow flowers visible through the doorway. Dad stepped in, looking very handsome. Excitedly, I exclaimed, "Oh, hi, Dad!"

He answered with a big smile, "Hi."

"What are you doing here?" I asked.

His eyes widened as he looked past me and he stepped forward. The back door had opened and a tall, beautiful, stately woman stepped up alongside Dad. His countenance lit up like a candle. I spoke, "Oh, Dad, don't you wish you could be married to her now?"

"Yeah" he grinned.

He reached out to her, and as Julie and Dad embraced each other, the whole room became a mass of vibrating golden white light. It encircled them very brightly, and I was also encompassed in the beauty and mutual love brought forth in this wondrous moment. Then Julie smiled and stated, "We have to go now."

I felt the vibrations speeding up again as the scene dissipated. Lying awake in bed, I smiled knowingly. Dad and Julie had met on the other side of life—on another level of living—in one of my Father's many mansions, and I was there to witness it.

Lourene Jurkovic

When you come to understand that God is our Father and Mother and that every one of us is a child of God, you come to understand God. When you come to understand that, if every one of us is a child of God, then we are all brothers and sisters, then you come to understand God.
　　　　　　　　　　　　　　　　　　　—In God's Truth

Dad

When my father was sixty years old, he died. There were no warnings, no good-byes. Although I was thirty-one, I felt as if my world had come to an end. Nothing made sense to me anymore, and the pain in my heart and soul went on and on.

I would constantly wonder, "Where did he go and why?" I was angry and torn with loyalty to my mom, who had endured his unceasing negativity and rotten disposition all their married life. Sometimes it had seemed that he never had a positive word to say to anyone except me. Oh, how I loved this man with his deep, resonant voice. We had a relationship that survived all transgressions.

Jonathan, my little boy, just four at the time, would see me walking around with tears in my eyes. "Are you sad about Grandpa?" he would ask. And as my heart was breaking inside, I would try to answer his innocent questions, trying hard not to scare him with information about the inevitable ending of our life on Earth.

I was left to mourn with Jonathan by my side, because the rest of the family was in southern California. I remember waking up many times from a dream about Dad. In my dreams, I would yell at him with anger, asking why he had left me. He would be sitting in the chair where he always sat, and all of a sudden, I would notice him watching me. I would tell him that he couldn't be there, because he was dead. Then I would start crying in my sleep with anguish and pain. This went on for years. My mother joined him in Heaven eleven months later. Now I was confused in my dreams. Was it my mom that was dead, or my dad, or was it both?

All I know is that my dreams helped to heal my breaking heart, and to know that they were both there helping me to mourn and to move on with my life.

Recently, I was on my bed thinking about a troubling situation in my life. I talked to my dad, cried a lot, and asked him to give me some guidance. I also needed to get a good night's sleep, since I hadn't slept well in weeks. All of a sudden, I felt my dad's strong arms around my shoulders and his whisper of love in my ear. Now I feel my dad's presence in my life more and more, and I thank God for His perfect wisdom in this life.

Julie Bennett

My Son's Dream

Three years ago, my husband, myself, and one of our three children moved from Wisconsin to Arizona, leaving all of our family and friends behind. Our oldest son stayed to continue with school in Illinois at Lewis University, and our daughter stayed to finish her senior year in high school. This was a very difficult move for me, but knowing that they were close to family as well as dear friends made it somewhat easier. The story I have to share comes from my son, Brad, nineteen, who moved in with my parents, Marlie and Til. He stayed with them during summers and school vacations.

My father, Marlie Gallagher, Brad's grandpa, suffered a stroke in the recovery room after surgery and died six weeks later. This is the story Brad shared with me:

When I tell the story about Grandpa, I usually give some background information, like how he taught me how to hunt and fish and how we became close while I was living with him and Grandma. He would share war stories and other stories of hunting and fishing trips and trips to his cabin. He would talk about Steel Forms, the construction company he started almost fifty years ago. He was involved with Steel Forms up until the day he had his stroke.

Because of how active he had been, it was hard to look at him in a hospital bed with all the tubes and hoses in him and to see him partially paralyzed. It hurt to see him that way, and you could see the pain and frustration in his eyes.

One summer night, I had a dream. I dreamt that I was in

the living room, kneeling next to Grandpa, who was sitting in his favorite La-Z-Boy. He wasn't lying back but was sitting upright, both hands on the armrests. He was dressed in his usual attire—khaki slacks and a button-down shirt. He was clean-shaven and had his hair nicely combed back, like he had just gotten out of the shower. He had a pleasant look on his face and there was a glow about him. He seemed very content, and did not say a word.

While I was still kneeling beside him, he raised his left hand and started moving his fingers around and rolling his wrist a little. I looked at him in amazement and said, "Grandpa, you can move your hand." I was amazed because he had been paralyzed for close to a month. He looked at me with a grin and gave me his patented wink, his way of saying everything was all right.

I had gotten that same wink a couple of days before his stroke. After dropping off some supplies, he had started down the road in his blue Dodge, and I had waved at him. He smiled and gave me the same wink I would see in my dream.

In the dream, after he winked at me, I heard the phone ring and I woke up. My first thought was that it was raining and my boss was calling to tell me not to come to work. Then I heard Grandma on the phone saying things like, "Oh my God. Really? I wasn't expecting this. Oh, God." So I knew something was wrong. I went out to see what happened, and after Grandma hung up the phone, she told me Grandpa had died.

I didn't think about my dream until the next day, and for some reason, I never cried when I remembered it. Maybe it was because in the dream, Grandpa smiled and winked at me, telling me everything was all right. At least I like to think so.

We buried my dad on August 2, 1997, on my sister's fortieth birthday. She was having a very difficult time with his death and prayed for a sign that he was okay and was with her. The day after the funeral, my sister, her husband, and three kids went to a family camp in northern Wisconsin, as they have done for a number of years. That evening, as part of the program for the children, a gentleman talked about birds of prey and showed one very special bird, a falcon, whose name was Marlie. My sister couldn't believe her ears, so she went up to the man and asked for the name again. Yes, it was Marlie.

Pam VanSlyke

The Balance

When I was seven, my parents divorced and my mother and I went to live with my grandparents. My grandfather became the father figure for me, and there was a close bond between us. Shortly before he died, I went to visit him. At the time, I was married and expecting my first child. Suddenly Papa—my grandfather—looked at me and said, "Do you really believe that the soul survives after you die?" I assured him that I did, and the conversation soon turned to other things.

The news of his death came during the week I was expecting my baby. Since I was having some problems with the pregnancy, the doctor said it would be best if I did not travel the 350 miles to attend his funeral. Several days following his death, I was thinking about him, and that night I had a dream in which he was reaching out to me. His face was contorted in pain, and he seemed to be searching.

I had read that we should pray for those who have passed over, just as we pray for the living. So I said a special prayer for Papa each night. A few days later, I had another dream about him, but this one was much different. I saw him riding a bicycle down the street where our old house was, and he was smiling, his white hair gleaming in the sun. He waved at me as he passed. I shouted, "Papa, wait for me," and started running after him. He shook his head no and kept going. I believe that my prayers helped him gain his balance (the bicycle) on the Other Side. So we should remember all those whom we have loved in our prayers—wherever they are.

Nona Bridge

White Picket Fences

When my grandmother died in 1992, I was pregnant with my daughter and it was an extremely hard time. We were all gathered around my grandmother in the nursing home, and it had been a long three days for her of waking and sleeping. I knew she was not suffering, as she seemed peaceful. Every so often, she would open her eyes, look up, smile with great joy, and open her arms wide as if to hug someone dear. Then she would fall asleep again. I knew she was seeing relatives who had passed on before her, and it made me so happy to know she had guidance for her crossing over.

Finally, after struggling for a few seconds, my grandmother crossed over as my sister and I held her hand. I told her to go ahead, it was time. I looked up towards the ceiling and smiled, saying, "Goodbye, Grandma." I knew she saw me and I was happy.

I often have vivid dreams of her in which I see her standing behind a white picket fence with green grass and blooming flowers. She always looks at me and smiles, and I know she is happy.

This past April I lost my cat, Foof. She was a dear friend and had been with me for seventeen years. I felt the loss deeply and it was lonely with out her; actually, it still is.

A short time later, I had another dream of my grandmother standing behind the picket fence, but this time, I felt she had something she wanted me to see. I noticed a furry little tail wrapped around her leg and as I watched, I saw my furry friend come around to the front and sit down. I felt so good to know that my grandmother and Foof were together on the Other Side waiting to welcome me when I crossed over. Some people do not believe animal spirits cross over to be with us, but I do. I am so looking forward to seeing them both again, my wonderful grandmother and my most treasured feline friend.

Angela James

The Picture

In July 1988, my lovely daughter Sonia, thirty-four, lost her battle with Hodgkin's disease. In the weeks that followed her passing, I wondered where she might be in her journey and if she was all right. One night, I had a dream, which to this day remains very clear and precise:

I was seated in an empty courtroom. As I sat waiting to see what was going to happen, a side door opened and my daughter walked in. She was radiant and more beautiful than she had been before the disease took its toll on her looks. She wore a big smile and glowed with happiness as she approached me, her shoulder-length ash blond hair turned neatly under. Her skirt billowed out around her knees as she walked. But even more noticeable to me than her looks and dress was the presence of angels.

They appeared as lovely young ladies who hovered around her, moving with her as she walked towards me. Sonia seemed unaware of them. They seemed to be clearing the way for her as she moved along as if she were royalty. If a hair slipped out of place, they tucked it in. When the folds of Sonia's skirt flared out, they gently pressed them back into place. I felt that the message to me was that she was all right, healthy, and happy, and that every need, no matter how trivial, was being met.

But I realized that being in this courtroom meant this was Sonia's "judgment" day. How could she look so happy, knowing that she might have to answer for her earthly shortcomings? I put the question to her. With a smile, she replied, "I'll just tell them that wasn't me." This was the end of my dream.

I understood her meaning. On Earth we are souls enclosed in a body. Once the body is shed, the soul can truthfully say, "That wasn't me."

Not long after the dream, I had another reassuring experience regarding my daughter's passing, this time while I was awake. I had gone shopping for groceries, and in the shopping center was a small pharmacy. As I parked my car, I felt an urge to go to the pharmacy even though I had no need of anything there. I silently protested, yet the pressure to go persisted, so I went.

Standing just inside the door, I thought, "Okay, I'm here. Now where do I go?" At the rear of the store was a section containing gift items, and I seemed to be directed there although there was no occasion coming up at which a gift would be required. I kept feeling the promptings, so I headed for the gift section. Once again, I thought, "Okay, I'm here. Now what?"

There was nothing I could do except look around. On a bottom shelf was a stack of pictures. The top picture caught my eye. I picked it up and studied it closely. It was not a picture that would appeal to everyone, but it spoke volumes to me.

In the center of the picture were two robed figures, one of whom was Jesus. His face could be seen as He embraced the other figure, whose face could not be seen. It was obvious that this was someone who had just passed over, and it seemed obvious to me that it was my daughter. There was a pained expression on Jesus' face, as if He were saying, "I'm so sorry for all you had to endure while on Earth."

Although the face of the other figure could not be seen, there seemed to be a sense of uncertainty and disbelief as she returned the embrace of her savior. Before passing over, Sonia had lost a considerable amount of weight, being hardly more than skin and bones. Chemotherapy had left her hair thin and wispy. The artist had captured it all so perfectly.

The background of the picture was clear blue sky, except for two cloudlike, upraised hands on either side. They seemed to be pronouncing a benediction over the scene as well as a welcome to this returning soul.

This picture has brought me much peace and comfort. I shudder to think what a blessing I would have missed if I had ignored the urging of my guardian angel. I know that my daughter is all right. I know she's happy. I know she's in good hands, and I know I will see her again.

Patricia C. Harcum

Part Five

Extraordinary Personal Stories

The following are personal stories that involve the transition of the spirit. In some of these extraordinary accounts, you will find the writers mentioning the number 444 and experiences they have had with that number.

The 444 phenomenon is extraordinary, for it has touched the lives of many thousands of people throughout the world. It was first mentioned in *The Messengers*, which described spiritual life experiences I have had. I was told through angelic intervention that 444 means the power of God's love, and that it would play a very important role in my life as well as provide witnesses to the spiritual experiences I was having.

Many of the 444 experiences related here fall into categories that are beyond the possibility of coincidence or have any explanation other than that the individuals experienced divine intervention in their lives.

Nick Bunick

Brad

In January of 1999, my nephew Brad killed himself. He was my sister Liz's oldest son and nineteen years old. He put a shotgun in his mouth and pulled the trigger.

Brad never cared much for me when he was little. I had moved away when he was just seven years old. When his mom died in 1995 and I was back in Louisiana for the funeral, Brad and I connected over the topic of Chevy trucks. He had one just like mine and was amazed that I knew as much as I did about parts and mechanics. Brad was fifteen at the time. I talked to him a couple of times after that, inviting him to come to Atlanta to see me. I would do anything I could to help him. I found out that the day he died, he had asked his grandmother (my mother) for my phone number, but he never made the call.

I drove across the country in my 1988 Blazer to attend his funeral. After I returned home, I got back to my usual routine. We run a family business, and I am on the road three to four hours a day doing various errands. I have a habit of listening to one cassette tape over and over for days. At this time it was an Elton John tape, and I had listened to it hundreds of times already. One morning while I was running my errands, the song "Sorry is the Hardest Word" came on. The words to that song are, "What do I do to make you love me? What do I do to make you care? What do I do when lightning strikes me and awake to find that you're not there?"

I heard a sad voice behind me say, "That's how I felt, Aunt Cheryl." I thought I was imagining things, and kept driving. On the other side of the tape is the song "Daniel." At the part in the song where he says, "I can see Daniel waving good-bye," I heard the voice behind me again saying, "Yeah, that happened." Daniel was Brad's brother.

I felt that someone was sitting in the backseat, leaning forward on my right and hanging his head in sadness at this last statement. I was sure I was losing it, but I decided to respond. Since I had been at the funeral and I had not seen Daniel wave to his brother, I thought he meant this figuratively. So I answered out loud, "You mean you saw him say good-bye at the funeral, don't you?" The emphatic reply came, "No! Say what I say."

I was shocked. Now the voice was talking back to me. I realized it was Brad. He had a temper, and I could feel a temper rising with the last statement. I kept quiet after this until the tape came back to the first song again. This time, Brad started talking very excitedly. He said I needed to do it soon. He begged me. I tried to explain that it would hurt his father and brother terribly if I told them this. How could I? They weren't open to it. They all always thought I was a little off anyway. This would just seem like I was causing undue pain. I couldn't do it. I didn't know how. I tried to think of some way I could relay his message without telling them Brad was in my Blazer when he talked to me.

This argument with Brad went back and forth for two weeks. His energy got stronger and stronger. I could feel him pushing against my right arm as I was driving, trying to convince me to deliver his message. He was like a child tugging on his mother's skirt saying, "Momma, Momma, Momma," until he gets her full attention. That's what I was feeling. His presence stayed in my truck most of the time. After two weeks, it started taking its toll on me. I hadn't told anyone what was happening, but everybody could tell something was wrong.

While I was standing in my kitchen preparing to leave in

my truck one more time, I knew I couldn't take it anymore. I knew Brad would start up with me once I was in the truck. It had gotten to the point where he was pushing me into the driver's door window while I was driving. People on the street were looking at me like I was a nut. I couldn't avoid the song on the tape. I had even tried to skip it, but there it would be, out of place on the tape. It even would play on the opposite side of the tape.

Finally, in order to keep my sanity, I stood in my kitchen and started yelling, "Okay! Okay! I'll do it! I'll tell your dad! I promise! But you have to promise me you'll move into the Light and do what you are supposed to. Brad, you know you're not supposed to be here with me. I promise to deliver your message, if you promise to move into the Light. Call on God, the angels, or your mom. They will be there for you. Just promise me."

At that very instant, I saw something I will never forget. In front of me, projected into the air, was a vision: Brad surrounded by the most beautiful angels. They encircled him completely, leading him away from me. The angels were a golden light that flickered and shone through them. The light seemed to come from inside them as if they were made of this light. Brad was looking back over his shoulder at me with a look that read, "Please don't let me down." How could I, after seeing that?

As the vision faded, I asked out loud, "Did this really happen? If it did, someone, please, give me a sign." At that instant, the phone rang. It felt like a response, and I was afraid to answer it, so I let the answering machine pick it up. It was a customer leaving a number for me to call. The number the lady left for me to call was 404-888-4444. You know the significance of 444s.

I delivered Brad's message. I wrote a long letter to Brad's dad. I even copied the tape for him. Basically, I just told him exactly what had happened to me and how it upset me, but that I had made a promise to Brad.

Several days later, his dad called me and said my letter

helped a little bit. We talked for a while, and to be honest, I could feel Brad's energy with me as we were talking, though I didn't tell his dad this. Later while I was talking to my mom, she told me how Brad's dad was saying he knew what I had said was the truth. There was one thing in my story that I had no way of knowing except through Brad. On the night Brad killed himself, as the ambulance was pulling away with his body in the early morning hours, no one was there except Brad's dad and his brother Daniel. And Daniel waved good-bye.

Cheryl Noland

*And when you provide love and compassion to your broth-
ers and sisters, you yourself are manifesting God.
When you come to understand that our bodies are nurtured by food and rest, but our spirits are nurtured by
experiencing love and compassion, then you come to
understand and know God.* —In God's Truth

Clear Prop

My father was a great guy. I kept being reminded of it as
family, friends, and even strangers came up to console me at
his wake five years ago. "What a great man," I heard over
and over again as the numbness of his death consumed me.
Sitting here today, I know I would have never dreamed of the
journey that I was about to undertake on that fateful day.

This is a story of one man's spiritual awakening, born out of
despair and depression. It is also a story of miracles, miracles that
were experienced by me, a regular guy. These were miracles
bestowed upon me by several gifted individuals who touched my
life, and who were instrumental in lighting up a life's path that I
didn't even know existed. My wish is that you can feel the same
hope through my story.

I had a typical childhood. My parents came out of
Brooklyn, New York, and moved the family to Long Island

in the 1960s. We lived a typical suburban middle-class life with its ups and downs. My mother was a housewife and my father was a manager for a manufacturing company. As I watched my father's life unfold, one thing was apparent to me: He could do it all. He was a friend, a big brother, a great carpenter, funny, compassionate, understanding, and a lousy fisherman. But most of all, he was my father, and we shared that silent bond that fathers and sons do, through thick and thin. I was his blood, and I didn't realize until he died how intertwined our lives were.

He was great at a lot of things, a renaissance man of sorts, but one world caught his fancy, and that was flying. He was obsessed with aviation. Model airplanes, jets, and rockets—if it took off, he wanted in. As a kid, I had fun watching him, because when he talked about airplanes, he became a kid again. He had that glimmer in his eye, that wild focus of someone with a calling. He just wanted to fly.

And fly he did. I will never forget the day he passed his aviation test and was given his private pilot's license. He was walking on air. I was eighteen and had never seen him so happy.

Through the haze of raising a family, he was able to reach a dream that he would not let die. He took me on his maiden flight out over Long Island Sound, even though secretly I was a white-knuckle flyer. Just before Dad started the engine of his rented Cessna two-seater, he belted out the pilot's clarion call: "Clear prop!" He was ready to fly off into his childhood dream. The family christened him with a new nickname, "Sky King," as we reveled in his accomplishment.

In the ensuing years, our family grew up. There were weddings, babies, anniversaries, birthdays, nine-to-five jobs, new homes, soccer games, and all the rest. My mother and father now had a daughter-in-law, two sons-in-law, and seven grandchildren. As Dad approached his mid-fifties, the pressures of executive life were taking their toll. He and my mother decided to retire to Florida and escape the New York rat race. It was tough on Mom being away from the kids, but as a couple, they were embarking on some of the happiest times of their married life. An extended family now, we spent less time together, but the quality was there when we did.

Dad got lucky. He discovered ultralight flying, which was very popular in Florida. In no time, due to his background as a pilot, he became rated as an instructor. He bought a two-seater plane and gave lessons to anyone who wanted to fly. He was living the dream, as his passion became his reality. I was down to see him for Thanksgiving week in November 1994. We spent some fun time together, and he invited me to the airport for a ride. I was still the greatest white-knuckle flyer around, but I went along anyway. "Clear prop," he yelled as we took off over Tampa Bay. His face was smiling in ecstasy as the wind blew through his hair. I, on the other hand, was terrified, filled with a sense of danger. I asked him to land immediately. He didn't hear me at first. I screamed at the top of my lungs, "Please land now!" We did, and safely, but here's where the story gets a little weird.

We walked back to Dad's car, and something came over me. He closed his door, and it just poured out of me. I was yelling at him. Don't you know how dangerous ultralight flying could be? What if you have an accident? What about your responsibilities, your liabilities, your house? What is going on here? For the only time in our lives, for that moment, I was the father and he the son. I sensed danger but I didn't know why. Dad started the car, and we headed home in silence.

Mom and Dad came up the next month for their Christmas visit, which had become a family tradition, and then headed back to Florida with the "snowbirds," senior citizens who go to the warmer climates during the winter months. When I spoke to Dad on February 4, he was in a great mood, moving ahead with plans for his ultralight instruction and flight school. I wished him well in his new endeavor.

On February 11, 1995, I got a frantic call from my mother. My father had been killed in a crash landing of his ultralight. A student who was with him survived with a broken leg and back injuries. It was later discovered that there was a structural weld fracture, causing the plane to become uncontrollable in the sky. My father, fifty-nine, was killed instantly upon impact.

In the months after this loss, our family was overwhelmed by grief. There were tearful phone calls, empty family gatherings, and depression. Even the grandkids seemed different, as if their innocence had been stained. Someone was missing at the dinner table when the holidays came around. Something was ripped out from under us and solid ground was nowhere to be found. There was medication, therapy, support groups, and the support of friends, but to my mother, my sisters, and me, it seemed there was no way out of the painful downward spiral.

I had always been a very confident guy, well respected in the business community. We were enjoying the fruits of a happy upper-middle-class life. It couldn't have been better. But now I was lost, unable to focus. I didn't care about business. I was in more pain than I could have imagined possible. I woke up angry every day and became more isolated. I was a shell of the person I had been, and I was afraid I would never find my way back. I was scared for the better part of two years. I prayed for an answer to my pain.

It was a Saturday morning when one of my wife's close friends gave me a book to read entitled *We Don't Die* by Joel Martin and Patricia Romanowski. She told me that several years earlier, she had lost her grandmother and had been devastated for some time. This book helped her, and she thought it could help me. I picked it up and could not put it down until I finished it the next day.

We Don't Die is the story of a gifted man on Long Island named George Anderson. George is a spirit medium. At that time, the term "spirit medium" was a new one for me, a concept I had never considered up until that moment. To my amazement, George recounted incidents in which he could communicate with a stranger's lost loved ones, and verify this communication with up-to-the-minute details. I realized that if this book was true, I was reading about miracles. Why hadn't I heard about this? Why wasn't this possibility made known to me through the Church? This book and its contents opened a huge door for me that led me into a room filled with lots of questions. I stepped in and started on my journey.

I had a typical Catholic upbringing, with baptism, communion, confirmation, marriage, catechism, brothers, nuns—the whole nine yards. My church attendance fell off as I got older, but I had a good working knowledge of my religion. We learned about many issues concerning life and how to live it, but when we got to the death part, we were going to either Heaven or Hell, and you had to have faith about that part. You get buried, and you have to have faith about it all. I found out, after losing my father, that faith is a great concept until you need to rely on it.

In the weeks after reading *We Don't Die*, my curiosity peaked. What if this concept of talking with the dead were true? That you could verify the existence of your loved ones in the next world? The concept amazed me. If this is true, shouldn't we all know about it? I was filled with questions and doubts, but kept my mind open. Then one evening, I was reading a spiritual newsletter I had picked up at the local health food store. There was a story about a local "sprit medium" named Kim, who had helped the author communicate with his murdered sister. Again, here was an amazing story, with verification, that a connection between this world and the next existed. That was it for me. I had to try it, even though I had reservations and fears. This wasn't taught by the Church, but I needed something to close the painful wound that had festered for too long. I called Kim and nervously made an appointment for the following Friday night.

My wife looked at me as if I had two heads when I told her what I was going to do. She had been to psychic parties for fun, but never anything like this. But she knew I was searching for something, so she supported me in my quest.

When I got to Kim's, I didn't know what to expect.

Black curtains and burning incense with sounds of chanting in the background? No, nothing like that. Kim is a beautiful young mother of two, with an understanding, friendly husband. She has a warm, knowing smile and looks like your next-door neighbor. She is the recipient of a wonderful gift from God.

Kim described to me that she was in contact with a male energy with the name Joe. That was my father's name, but at the moment, I thought it could be a lucky guess since my name was Joe also. She had a second male energy with him, an older man with gray hair, named Tom. This startled me. My grandfather had passed on shortly before my Dad; his birth name was Salvatore, but his nickname was Tom. Kim was on to something.

She asked me if the name Abbey had any meaning to me. She said that my father was telling her that it was okay for Abbey to sleep on the bed. Kim looked puzzled.

Abbey was the name of a small dog that we had gotten my mother to keep her company after my father passed away. That week, my mother had mentioned to me that Abbey was sleeping in the bed with her.

I was amazed. It was happening. These were minute details of verification that no one else could know. Kim went on. Your father is laughing about the new blacktop on your sister's driveway. He thinks it's a riot. Again, Kim looked at me for verification, and at that point, I was blown away. Two weeks earlier, my sister and I had been laughing about a driveway blacktop job my brother-in-law had done just before a rainstorm. His work ended up floating in the street! Kim laughed at the story and the detail of verification.

After giving me several more unbelievable personal connections, Kim explained that she was clairaudient, and that "spirit" wanted to give me some guidance. Kim saw me reading many books in the near future, but noted that spirit wanted me to read a book entitled *The Messengers* by Julia Ingram, about the life of Nick Bunick. I jotted this down as Kim continued her reading with compassion and understanding.

When she was done, I knew that I had witnessed something special, a miracle. She had shown me, without a doubt, that my father and other loved ones were with us every day, in a specific way. I was very moved.

As I pulled away from Kim's house, I felt like the weight of the world was lifted off my shoulders. I was smiling from ear to ear, something that I hadn't done for two years. I felt hope for the first time. The words "clear prop" popped into my mind. Maybe I could "take off" again and move forward with my life.

I'm a businessman and I know that if someone gives you a lead, you have to jump on it. I had gotten a lead from Kim and "spirit" to read *The Messengers*, so I did. I could not put the book down, and somehow I knew that what I was reading was the truth. Its candidness about the difficulties in moving down a spiritual path as we relate to those around us and how they perceive us rang true with me as my own spirituality was coming to the forefront in my life. This was a book I could relate to.

What I didn't know at the time was that I would get verification of my feelings. About two months after reading the book, I was in a deep sleep and heard my Labrador retriever, Rags, give out one sharp bark. I jumped up and looked at the digital clock. It was 4:44, and I knew that this was no coincidence. I couldn't believe it, but with the course of events in my life now, I couldn't deny it either. This was the first of many 444 experiences I was to be blessed with, and I considered each one a miracle.

Before writing this story, I had a phone conversation with Kim, with whom I hadn't spoken in over a year. She felt that I would be writing my story, and that there was some connection to Nick Bunick's work that I would be hearing about. When I checked The Messenger Web site that evening, I was surprised to see Nick's request for material for his new book.

When I get a lead, especially from "spirit," I jump on it.

Joe Deflorio

Be Not Afraid

I am responding to your request for stories on death that could be helpful to others. The following is a near-death experience I had while I was a graduate student in molecular biology.

I was playing baseball on the "physiology" team. Jim was playing third base, and I was playing second and I was really hot. Suddenly, there was a line drive right over my head and I rocketed up into the air and snagged it. It was instinct and I was psyched, as people gave me lots of positive feedback for my playing.

Then a guy rifled a shot to my right side, striking the dirt two feet off my right foot. I crouched down, but as there was no way I could reach the ball with my right foot, because I was so psyched, I reached for it with my bare right hand. I stuck my hand down as fast I could and hit the dirt with it, jamming my finger hard into the ground. I stopped the hit and the ball bounced off my hand.

That is how I broke my finger the first time. The doctor said it was a "classic" spiral fracture. At the hospital, they put my finger in a metal splint to protect it. A few days later, I was trying to fix a lamp on my big desk. I was cutting wire on the cord to put a new plug in when the knife let go and I smashed my finger on the edge of the desk. I broke my finger again and had to go in for surgery.

I ended up needing three pins to put my finger together. It was a horror story. The nurses were all saying this operation was illegal. There were two student doctors and a professor working on my hand, drilling on my finger. They were saying things like, "Oh no, damn, oh well . . . too bad . . . can't find the C clamp."

They put a tourniquet on my arm, and when it was taken off, I could feel the blood flow back into my arm. My arm was cold. I could feel the warmth trickle back in from my shoulder and percolate down my arm and the nerves came alive again.

After the operation, my wife took me to our favorite restaurant to eat a steak. When I started to pass out at dinner, the maitre d' helped me to the car.

The bone in my finger was regenerating, starting to push the pins out. I went back to the hospital and showed them. Now I was back in the hospital for the second time in three weeks. They were going to cut my finger open and take the pins out. It was in the middle of the day and the clinic was busy; everyone was in a hurry.

They gave me a local injection of Xylocaine in the elbow. It was to make my arm numb from the nerve down. They missed, and it did not work right. The doctors were in a hurry and wanted to start cutting. I said I did not think it was numb. They said it soon would be.

I was conscious. They started to cut and it still hurt. "Oh, it will be numb soon," and they continued cutting. They decided to give me more Xylocaine. They injected it into my elbow and then immediately started cutting again. It hurt and I got upset.

Suddenly, I was in a state of blackness with my eyes closed, but I was still conscious. Soon, my body began to shut down, and I was aware my lungs and heart stopped. It was unusual, not like a sleeping state when your breathing and heartbeat are in the background. When your breathing and heartbeat stop, you realize this background noise is gone and it is more quiet than you ever knew it could be.

In my last conscious moment, I heard myself say, "Oh damn." I heard myself think, "Those may be the last words you ever utter and that is not a very classy was to go. Not like Butch Cassidy and the Sundance Kid when they jumped off the mountain."

Meanwhile, it was getting darker. It was changing from gray to black, then to black velvet, but there was not a hint of white. I knew I could not speak or think anymore. My awareness came through intuition. In fact, I had an overwhelming awareness, a certainty. It was more certain than my own name. I knew I had been there before, and I knew I had nothing to fear. I experienced a deep peace.

I was in a place of love. I could feel the love all around me. It was a pleasure, like an electric field, this field of love. I was in good hands. I was being cared for, and no harm would come to me. I was okay.

There was a point of gold light against the intense blackness in the distance. It started out as a pinpoint and then turned into a gold ball. I was moving towards that gold spot. As I started to move, I realized I was in a tunnel with no walls, yet there was no feeling of motion. It did not take very long to be drawn. I was very comfortable. I knew that there was nothing to be afraid of.

As I got closer, the gold spot resolved itself into recognizable shapes and figures. Two figures were standing side by side, a short one on the left, a tall one on the right—two men in gold robes. Their faces and skin were also soft gold. Between them was something on wheels like a golden hospital trolley. I wondered why anything in this dimension would have wheels.

I knew with certainty that if I reached them, I would be put on this wagon and they would escort me off to their left. I knew I would go to the left into another dimension that existed behind a black wall.

The men wore robes. I was shocked to recognize the face of the shorter one. He looked like the figure on the cover of my undergraduate philosophy book. Neither expressed emotion, both were impassive and calm.

I was being pulled back quickly and then upwards, like a

plane coming out of a dive. I started moving through layers of blackness. The two men faded off in the distance, and I kept rising through a gradient blackness that got lighter and lighter—normal black, then to gray-black.

When I reached the level of blackness I was used to—such as you see before you fall asleep—my lungs restarted. It got grayer, and then I opened my eyes and looked at the ceiling. No one was in the room but the doctor. He was at my left side with his back to me. I made a noise and he jumped. Startled, he turned to me. He was shocked. I think I said, "What happened?" He responded, "We thought we lost you. I was just putting the equipment away."

For the past twenty-five years, my wife and I have shared this story with many people who seemed troubled over death or the death of a loved one. It always brings relief to the listener as well as a new awareness of the subject of death.

I was very moved by the love and peace I found in my experience, as well as the feeling that there is nothing to be afraid of. Perhaps this is what the angels are trying to tell us when they say, "Be not afraid."

Peter Oates

Overwhelming Love

An understanding of death came for me when I had a near-death experience at fifteen. I had contracted spinal meningitis, and while lying down, I quietly left my body and hovered over it thinking, "I lived in there!"

Then I left, going through a window glass, and wondered how I had done that. I saw I had no legs, or arms, or body. I could see the beautiful blue sky and puffy white clouds, and suddenly I had an overwhelming feeling of love, more love than I had ever experienced. My childhood had not been a loving or comfortable one up to that time. I did not know about the spirit world, nor did I have a concept of God at that time.

When I felt this enormous love, I said to myself, "I never want to go back. I want to stay here!" I was enjoying hovering in one place when suddenly I was back on my couch inside my body.

Very disappointed, I said to myself, "Oh, I don't want to be here. I want to be there." Then I was hovering outside of my body again in spirit. Seconds later, just as quickly, I was back in my body. I never had that experience again. Now I am glad I returned. I am a mother of two sons and a daughter, and I have become a grandmother to a grandson and two granddaughters.

Thirteen years ago, I left organized religion and searched within for the truth through meditation and prayer. I found profound books like *The Messengers*, *A Course in Miracles*,

Mary's Message to the World, and *The Urantia Book.* Yet the religion I left was important in getting me to that place. I learned about God and His words about how to treat our fellow men, and I read the Bible cover to cover seven times, giving me a wonderful background for which I am grateful.

I have no fear of death after my experience in 1941 at age fifteen. I love to spread spiritual loving thoughts to everyone on Earth, and look forward in these exciting times to the great tomorrow.

Lovingly,

Claire Weissman

The Service

My husband had been ill for a number of years, and at one time suggested that since I was an ordained minister, I should consider conducting his funeral. I was not comfortable doing this, and upon his transition I called on my teacher, a well-known minister, to conduct the chapel portion of the service. An associate pastor I knew desired to do the graveside service, so arrangements were made for him to do that.

During the five-mile trip to the veterans' cemetery, the associate pastor's automobile stalled. We had all gathered at the gravesite, but now there was no pastor to conduct the service. After waiting fifteen minutes, the funeral director announced that we had to begin.

My daughter said, "Mom. You must do the service. Dad must want you to do it." With no other option, I proceeded to conduct the graveside service. Upon our returning home, the associate pastor called me and said, "My car just quit and I couldn't get it started. After I realized that the service must be over, I gave up, and wouldn't you know it, the car started. I took it to the garage and they checked the car over and could find no problem whatsoever." He added that he also "had a feeling" that I was supposed to do this service.

I do not believe that what transpired was a coincidence. I believe that my husband's spirit had a hand in this event so that I would officiate at his burial. No one will ever convince me that death is annihilation. I know that my husband intervened at his own funeral. There is much more to us than we realize. Death is only a transition of who we are as a mortal body into a spiritual body. I pray that you also understand this and embrace it into your own mind and heart.

Reverend Doris Roser

We Truly Are Spirits

Her stomach was bloated. My mother told me that she was just as large as when she had been pregnant with me. Only this time, on Halloween night in 1984, my mom gave birth to a "baby" tumor the size of a grapefruit. From there, she seemed to slip away from us.

My mother spent most of her time ill from chemotherapy treatments and antihormonal pills. Not only did she lose her hair, but she felt as though she had lost her womanhood. Every time she went to the hospital to have lab work done, she would come back even more depressed. The lab results continually foretold a grim future.

A part of her felt that she was spiraling downward with no control. My mother worried deeply not only about her condition, but for my sister and me. My mother had faith, and I was told I would be fine, but my sister was a different story. At the time of my mother's sickness, Kim, my sister, was in New Hampshire at a school for the disabled. Kim was not applying herself as she should. My mother worried about Kim's future. She was not certain that everything would be okay with Kim if something serious happened to her.

One day, I came home from school and entered the house. There seemed to be an air of relief and peace surrounding my mother that day. She knew that I was different and that I had a deep faith, so she shared with me what had happened to her on the way home from the doctor's office that changed her outlook and gave her hope for my sister. As she drove praying to God, a multistory-high Jesus appeared in front of the car with my sister at His feet. He told her that everything would be okay. From that moment on, a sense of peace permeated her being when it came to my sister. My mother died of ovarian cancer a couple of weeks later. My sister is now a productive member of society and has a great life.

It was just after my mother's death that I had my first spiritual visitation. I was riding home with my uncle from the hospital, and it was still early in the morning. My mom had passed on a couple hours earlier. I was talking to God and Mom. I asked if my mother was still there to give me a sign, as I stared at the sky that crisp spring morning. Clouds hung like wisps of cotton candy from the heavens. As I gazed at them, one cloud separated from a much larger one and took the form of an angel. It formed a body, then wings, then it flew off. I had no doubt then or now that my mother is fine and living.

The second of many angel encounters happened when my twenty-two-month-old son passed away. It was five days after the Oklahoma City bombing, and I remember I had said then, "I could never handle losing a child; it would kill me." My heart aches for families who lose a child. I was devastated by my own son's death. To this day, we have no known reason for his death. He just died.

My family and I traveled to Connecticut for his wake and burial. His body arrived shortly after. I went to a local store to buy him a hat and some mementos. I felt as though I would suffocate in the store, so I left and sat on the curb in front of the parking lot. There in my pain and anguish, my face washed with tears, I stared at the sky, asking why. I was not angry with anyone, God or myself. I just wanted to know why.

Just then, just as I searched for answers I believed I would never find, an angel fifty feet tall descended from the sky. The angel was the most beautiful pure white. It ascended upwards, enveloped in a lovely pink, and disappeared. I was then assured of my son's afterlife and the deep love I felt from my son, and my father/mother encompassed me. God has never forgotten me in my pain. I have never been alone on this journey. My angels have shown their presence to me in tragedy and in joy. I am blessed by their strength and their reminders of my strength. There is no death, only life beyond our eyes. We are spirits having a human experience.

Marsha D. Kennedy

The Soul Departs

To understand mourning is to understand the different emotions that are a part of mourning. Just as there are multiple pieces to a puzzle that make up the whole picture, so too is the emotional makeup of mourning the result of several different emotions. When all is said and done, what we are feeling is more about ourselves than for the soul passing on to another plane. I do not mean this critically, but this is my foundation for how I deal with death. I hope that this view will provide another option for those consumed by mourning.

My first experience with death came when I was two years old. I don't remember a lot about my uncle Leroy, but I do remember the intense love I had for him, as well as the sadness when I understood that I would not be able to spend time with him again. Death was an unwelcome separation, and I wanted to die as well so that I could be with him. I voiced this sentiment often until I was seven, when my mother stated how much it upset her. There were other deaths in the family, but none would be as profound for me as my mother's passing.

My mother was the glue that held our family together. She was a short, feisty Irish woman with a strong sense of direction. She had been forty-one when she gave birth to me, and I constantly worried about her dying. I did not want to be separated from her as I had from my uncle. She would often reassure me that she wasn't going anywhere. These were the same last words she spoke to me in her life.

It was five days after my thirtieth birthday, and the day

started out like any other Saturday. Chores were done, the apartment was cleaned, and I spoke with Mom on the phone. My daughter was spending the night at her friend's house. I didn't have a clue as to what would happen later that night. I woke up Sunday to a phone call from my sister saying that Mom had had a stroke and was in the hospital.

For the first time in my life, I saw my mother not only in a hospital bed, but unable to move or see. The doctors told us that a piece of arterial plaque had broken free from a blood vessel somewhere and lodged near the base of her brain. They asked us if she was an organ donor, as her prognosis was that she wouldn't make it. If she could live through the first three days after this stroke, then her chances for a limited existence were dramatically increased. Mom, being the feisty Irish woman that she was, made it three days and some, to Wednesday.

I had been with her at the hospital since Sunday, then I went home to shower. I had just gotten home when my sister called to say Mom had had another stroke when they put the feeding tube down her throat. That was my initiation into Hell. I saw my mother struggle and fight for fifty-four hours before she passed on. Then I stayed with her body for four hours and followed the hearse that carried her remains to the mortuary. I was consumed with anger that God didn't make her passing easier. She had had a rough life and at the very least deserved to pass peacefully. I was consumed with fear. Who was going to catch me if I fell? Who was going to love me like she did when things happen, and whom could I trust to tell? I knew she was free from the earthly challenges and turmoil and I knew no one deserved that freedom more, but I also knew that we wouldn't be able to do things together like we had done before. Everything would change, and with these emotions came the tears.

I want to share something with you. I can't tell you how I got this information, just that I did and that I believe it to be true. My mother was not in her body at the end. She did not feel what her body was doing in the death process. When I received this information, I was told that this is often the case. The body has to go through a process in which it ceases to function, but the soul of the person does not have to be present for the end to occur.

This took place seven years ago. Yes, I still miss her, but I have learned to appreciate those times when she makes her presence known, those times when I see someone who looks a lot like her; or when we are together in my dreams; or when I look at my hand and see her hands. I am happy for her, but I still wish there was a long distance number I could call to reach her.

As far as the fear, I am lucky to have two daughters and a loving husband, and I focus on them and try to remember every day to thank God for them. Someone once said that the only certainty in life is change. I think there is always fear with the unknown, and I'm just learning to have the courage to face it head-on. The anger was the hardest hurdle for me, and if it weren't for my guys—my angels—I would probably still be there, angry.

If one analyzes the emotions one feels regarding death—whether it is the death of a parent, a sibling, a spouse, a friend, or a child—they are about how we feel at the loss of their physical presence. But the soul never dies, so our loved ones live on.

Colleen Covey

*L*ove is the greatest manifestation of God one can give to another and one can receive from another. If every one of us in the world embraced love, we would not have wars, we would not have prisons, we would not have hungry children, we would not have abused women, for none of these things could exist in a world filled with love.

—In God's Truth

Joshua's Lighthouse Angels

Joshua, my son, is now in spirit. He was called home on January 12, 1997. At the time of his passing, Josh was a twenty-one-year-old college senior at St. Mary's College of Maryland, and he worked part-time at Piney Point Lighthouse. Josh and his roommate, John Taylor, were killed instantly when their car hit a tree during an ice storm. Of course, we were devastated.

About two months after the accident, we met a woman named Jayne Howard. Jayne lives not far from us, and through friends of a friend who had heard of us and the terrible condition we were in, the angels sent Jayne to us. Jayne helped us be open to the possibility that angels exist and wait to help us if we only ask.

That was the beginning of a magical transformation in my life. The angels directed me to a wonderful and humbling service, the creation of Joshua's Lighthouse Angels. We began to get signs from Josh in the form of images of lighthouses that he was okay. That is any parent's first concern, and Josh knew that. Then came the nonstop inspiration to open a place where bereaved parents could come to share, grieve, and hope, and understand that there is no such thing as death, that our children are as close to us after death as they have ever been while alive.

With the help of my new best friend, Jayne, Joshua's Lighthouse Angels opened on November 1, 1997, ten months after Joshua's passing. This was a miracle, because I was in no condition physically or emotionally to take on such a task, but I made an agreement with the angels that I would do this if they would show me the way.

Since then, in a short period of time we have moved to a larger location, have hosted a daylong workshop with James Twyman (author of *Emissary of Light*), have been featured on every local news station, and have been invited to exhibit at the Whole Life Expo in March 1999. It is no coincidence that Nick Bunick as well as Jimmy Twyman were at the Expo. It is all in divine order. Also, 444 keeps coming at me nonstop at exactly the moment when I need it most. So I offer the angels a huge thank you. I giggle with joy and go about my business when it happens.

The following poem was written by the angels through Jayne Howard.

Joshua

Joshua Dansicker was a typical boy doing
all the things earthly children did,
those around him were never conscious
of the pair of golden wings he hid.

He grew in character
as he grew in height,
and at twenty-one he spread his wings
and his soul took flight.

Joshua answered the call from the
Lighthouse Angels to serve from afar.
On a fateful evening he would leave
his earthly body in the crash of a car.

Joshua had worked on Earth
as a keeper of the Light,
while a senior at St. Mary's College, working
to keep Piney Point Lighthouse shining bright.

His service would continue on January 12, 1997,
when Joshua joined the Heavenly Host;
as a keeper of a heavenly lighthouse
he would fill a divine post.

For in heaven there are lighthouses that shine upon us
when we feel alone in the dark,
lighthouses that guide our path when we feel
forsaken and the presence of hope seems stark.

This store is a result of Joshua and his lighthouses
beaming from above,
for after Joshua's death his parents began
receiving signs of his presence and love.

Whenever Josh's family felt
as if their grieving hearts would break,
there would appear a sign of a lighthouse
they could not mistake.

Though they no longer saw Joshua
as the son or brother they knew,
there always appeared a lighthouse on a truck
or a license plate or in a magazine right in their view.

And through the lighthouses they heard Joshua
ask them not to stand by his grave and weep,
"For I am serving God,
and I have a lighthouse to keep."

Mary Dansicker

Trials and Lessons

I am now sixty-four years young and have had many miraculous experiences on my bumpy journey through life. Each has brought me to where I am today, with a wonderful peace inside knowing God is constantly working in my life, letting me know that it is His way, not my way!

The story I wish to share with you took place when I was forty-five. Over the years, I had been both close and distant to my path of spiritual awareness. I came back to the Church in my late thirties, feeling I needed to get close to God again, as I had been in my younger years. I felt good that I had a need in my life to reunite with my religion, and I began to practice and study the word of God. It seemed I had a hunger or a void inside me that needed to be filled. I jumped in to study again, soaking up all I could retain as God's knowledge came my way. I knew I was on a spiritual high, and I knew I had tapped into my third dimension. I had already experienced physical and mental achievements, but now I was fulfilling the greatest of all. My dormant spiritual soul was coming alive.

In March of 1980, my daughter Karen was ready to give birth to my first grandchild and my mother's first great-grandchild. My family was anxious to welcome this new addition. My mom, myself, and my daughter had been very close over the years. However, since my mom and dad spent the winter months in Los Angeles with my brother, she would not be here to share the last months of pregnancy. Even so, we talked constantly on the phone to update Mom on all the news.

In February, all the unseen events started to take place. First my dad went into the hospital with a mild heart attack (he had had many over the years). Then my brother was admitted with hepatitis, and he had eleven liver specialists trying to figure out a treatment for a rare strain of hepatitis.

The telephone calls started to fly back and forth with updates of their conditions. Next, within a week, my mother also ended up in the hospital with pneumonia, or so the doctors thought. So I had three of my loved ones in the hospital at the same time. They put a portable monitor on my mother and found out she needed to have triple bypass surgery. Here I was at home in Chicago, having planned a big baby shower for Karen, and feeling that maybe I would not have a mom, dad, or brother to share this great event with since all three of them were in life-threatening situations.

My mom, being the strong one of the family, talked me out of flying to Los Angeles to be with them. Her argument was that she wanted to have the surgery in Los Angeles. She had been consulting with the best specialists in the field. I would be better off waiting a week to come to Los Angeles and I would be needed more when they got home from the hospital. My mom was to have the surgery on Wednesday, Karen's shower was on Saturday, and I would fly out the following week after Mom's release. Her vital signs were good and her team of doctors had never had a fatality.

Of course, my newfound faith was being tested to the fullest. I was in constant prayer, asking for God's guidance in all these major decisions. I felt strong, even though my mental thoughts and emotions were being stretched to the point of breaking.

On the day of the surgery, I attended my Bible study group at church and we prayed for God to guide my mother through her operation. As the day wore on, my church friends were calling me with support, which gave me a peace of mind. My dad and brother were to shoulder her decision to be operated on right away. Although my life was in chaos, I remember having a calm feeling that day that everything was in God's hands and that we would be all right. It was a long day, and it was not until around five that afternoon that my brother called to let us know that, indeed, all was well. Mom was in the intensive care unit and doing great. We had passed the crisis. I was filled with joy. That sealed it right then and there that the credit, knowledge, and thanks all went to God. My faith took a huge leap forward. I then knew how great the power of prayer was and that I had all the answers.

I went to bed joyfully exhausted from the events of the last couple of weeks. My dad was doing better, and though my brother was not out of the woods yet, my mother would be coming home. I would be at the baby shower Saturday and the next week I would be in Los Angeles to help my loved ones recuperate.

All of a sudden, I woke up in the middle of the night. A feeling came over me I cannot explain. I got up and looked at the clock. It was around three-fifteen. Uneasy for some reason, I made some toast and tea. I felt a presence with me that I did not recognize and did not want to acknowledge. I said to myself, go back to sleep, you are just overreacting from all the stress. I returned to bed and fell into a sound sleep. At six-thirty, I woke up to the phone ringing and my brother's voice. My mother had suffered a hemorrhage around three A.M. our time and she had died. From the autopsy, we later discovered that the surgery had been a success, but the hemorrhage had occurred from a lacerated heart. The team of doctors had had their first fatality.

Even as I write this years later, I am crying, reliving the pain of hearing those words of my brother telling me what had happened. He said he had not wanted to call in the middle of the night so that I might at least get one good night's sleep before having to face another stretch of sleepless nights ahead. Her funeral now faced us. I told him I would fly out at once.

I had known before my brother told me that my mother was dead. I knew it when I woke up at three that her spirit was with me, and I knew as well that an unknown presence was around me. But I did not want to accept my intuition.

Then came the second shock. "How could you, God, let me think my mother was fine and then take her from me?" The anger that flooded me was as deep as or deeper than the feeling of my new faith. I felt betrayed, bewildered, and wounded. My new spiritual legs were cut off. I faced the days ahead bitter and angry as if I had been robbed of all common sense, putting my life in God's hands instead of using my own mental abilities.

I proceeded to Los Angeles, realizing this would be the first time I would have to make funeral arrangements for someone. My grief was overwhelming, but I knew I had a job to do. My dad and brother put me in control because of my insurance background (I had been in the insurance business for ten years), knowing I would be capable of dealing with the arrangements. Of course, they were in no physical condition to deal with any of this. We planned to have the funeral in Indiana.

When I arrived with my son Jeff at the hospital, to our shock, my brother was coming down the hall looking very yellow. He already had told the doctor he was leaving for Indiana to bury his mother. The doctor said he was not to leave, that he could have severe complications and could die. The hospital refused to release him, so he just walked out.

We went to my father's room, and he too was told he could not be released. The cold winter air would be bad for his lungs and the shock of his wife's death was too much for him to handle in his weakened condition. He informed the doctor that he had been with his wife Peggy since he was eighteen and that where she went, he went.

The following days were a blur. We had a wake for my mother and would be shipping her body back to Indiana for another wake and then to her final resting place. On the plane, I sat with a weakened father, a sickly brother, and my mother in a coffin. My twenty-four-year-old son was with me, finding out about the realities of life and death.

My mother's body was to be shipped to Indianapolis, then picked up by the hearse and taken to the funeral home in Logansport. After we got to O'Hare airport, it would take a couple of hours before we would arrive at my house. After that, there would be another two-hour drive to my parents' retirement home in Indiana, which was about thirty minutes from the funeral home. The weather was blisteringly cold, windy, and dreary, and was especially unpleasant after sunny Los Angeles.

We were exhausted when we arrived at my parents' home, which had to be opened up and the water and furnace turned on, since everything had been shut off for the winter. I now had the support of my husband, my youngest son Keith, and my oldest son Jeff, as well as the help of my mother's sisters and families. Most of this time was a blur, as I was whipped emotionally and physically. I think my anger at God is what kept me going.

Of course, I missed the baby shower, and since Karen was due in another three or four weeks, we felt it best that she come down to Indiana on the day of the burial, for she too was going through a terrible emotional loss.

There were so many people at Mom's funeral, I think the whole town turned out. The Ladies Guild, which my mother belonged to, wanted to take care of the lunch at the church after the burial. They informed us a tree would be planted by the church in my mother's name; today this tree stands fully grown on the spot.

The night before the burial, we were up very late. My dad and brother had me worried. I kept feeding my brother juices, and my dad would not keep his scarf over his mouth when he was in the cold air. He was so drained by then, I didn't want him to have another heart attack. Again, my anger at God kept me going.

We were all tired but went to bed to get a good night's sleep, for the next day would be a long funeral procession to the cemetery. I called my daughter to tell her to bundle up, for she was to arrive in the morning for the burial.

As I crawled in bed, I cried from grief, exhaustion, and anger. Every emotion came up, and each hit me hard. I was as low as I had ever felt in my life, and I do not know when I fell asleep. I was totally spent. Not knowing if I was dreaming or if the phone was ringing, I got up in a daze, wondering who was calling in the middle of the night.

It was again three in the morning. The voice on the other end was my son-in-law informing me I was a grandma to a fine little boy. Karen was doing fine, and my mother became a great-grandmother on the day she was to be buried. We were to find out later that Michael Eugene Rose had been born at the same time my mother died.

At that moment, a miracle occurred. God spoke to me. "I can take away life and I can give life." Immediately, all my anger was gone, and I was filled with an overwhelming peace and knowledge that He was with me even though I denied Him. He forgave me, and I experienced my first of many lessons in universal law, which I never questioned again through life as I faced other trials of my faith. God be with you too!

Shirley Essenberg

My Spiritual Journey

I had a special talent for art that was surfacing during my formative years, and my parents beamed with pride as many drawing and art awards and acknowledgments came my way.

In our class of fifty students, there was one extraordinarily talented artist named Lonny. Even as a boy of ten, he had a style and ability that could put Picasso to shame. Undoubtedly, it was our mutual love of art and our continuous praise and encouragement of each other that cemented the close bond of friendship between us. But something else about Lonny attracted me to him, which set him apart from the rough-and-tumble image I had of most of the boys I knew.

Lonny was good. Not "goody-good," but just plain good, through and through. He was gentle, warm, friendly, positive, and abundantly kind to everyone; and I suppose that's why I thought it so unfair when he was targeted by a swarm of bees the following summer, the aftereffects of which proved fatal to him by the spring of 1948. I was thirteen years old.

Sweet, endearing Lonny was the first person close to me who died. He was the first person who brought the reality and terror of death into the core of my being; the first person who made me acutely aware that I too would someday die. He was the first person who taught me how unexpectedly brutal life can be; the first person to cause intensely growing doubts in me of the sanctity and validity of the

Christian Church and its dogma, and the God it proclaimed. Most important, Lonny was the first person who turned my life so topsy-turvy that neither I nor my parents knew who I was anymore.

Even though I had been a good kid up until that point, I became bitter and defiant, sarcastic and incorrigible, disobedient, distant, and destructive. I couldn't count the number of times my exasperated mother would wring her hands and remark, "What's happened to you?" But I'd only shrug my shoulders and retreat to my room or storm out of the house, never stating where I'd be going or when I'd be back.

The next couple of years, our house was like a war zone, and the escalating conflict revolved around me. Unlike in most families, both of my parents were strong-willed and independent, with neither being the dominant or submissive partner. In most instances, I greatly admired this quality in them, but because each took an opposing viewpoint where I was concerned, I felt more like a fraying rope in a tug-of-war than a human being. Mother's solution was to tighten the rope, Dad's was to loosen it. By the time I was fourteen, Mother deferred to Dad's psychological approach in handling me.

Dad had a knack for taking a negative and transforming it into a positive. As an example, he did not try to instill a sense of guilt and shame by putting me down for my outbursts against religion and the Church. Instead, he'd say, "Good. That's good that you're questioning," or, "I can see what you mean," or, "You've got a point there." He'd use logical, intelligent persuasion, never force; encouragement and praise, never criticism and condemnation. If he didn't know the answer to the more profound issues I'd present, he'd say so and not pretend otherwise. He'd say he believed there was an answer to everything, and if finding it was that important to me, it was up to me, not him or anyone else, to persevere until I did! He never passed the buck when I'd confront him with evidence I found that justified my sense of betrayal and mounting distrust of the Church or its teachings, such as the fourth commandment, which stated,

r thy father and mother that thy days may be long
he land which the Lord thy God giveth thee."

"See, Dad!" I'd proclaim. "That's an out-and-out lie, because nobody ever honored and obeyed his parents more than Lonny, and his days were short!" To my wonderment, Dad not only agreed but stood up for me then and thereafter whenever, using good reason from evidential data, I challenged any kind of established, conventional authority.

Thus, by the closing of my fourteenth year, some semblance of order and harmony was restored in our household. The air rang with music once again as my dad strummed his guitar and sang the old sad ballads that brought tears to my eyes, or as the weekly get-together of his barbershop quartet filled the house with melodious voices, songs, and laughter, echoing into the night after I'd gone to bed. The stereo blared with my mother's growing collection of records, while other times her fingers flew across the keyboard of the old upright piano, producing wonderful music. She was an accomplished pianist and music teacher.

I resumed my extroverted, energetic, and creative lifestyle, with one significant change. Some childlike part of me had died with Lonny—my blind faith. With this death came introspection and a fervent desire to find the truth, no matter what the price. A price, I soon learned, that would require the ultimate!

During the early part of my fifteenth year, I lay awake one night pondering the major changes that had transpired in me since Lonny's death. I reflected on how this one event had thrust me from the confines of a sheltered "playpen" type of existence into the realities and uncertainties of the world. It made no difference to me if my life was ripe and wonderful when I knew that others' lives were not. Pain, suffering and grief, toil, struggle, and survival—these seemed to be the lot of mankind. Despite what brief achievements each person made during their life, the result for all was the same—deterioration, disease, and death. What was the point to it all? None, as far as I could see. It was as ludicrous as a man spending the best years of his life building an elaborate, beautiful mansion, and then setting a torch to it when he was finished. Life—it was nothing other than a futile, cruel joke, I cynically concluded.

Finally, while lying on my back, eyes closed and arms comfortably by my side, I relinquished the battle and resigned myself to the fact that if it were possible, I would willingly allow myself to die to find out what death was like. How? Certainly not by suicide, as that thought never entered my mind. But by beseeching Jesus to grant me this request to experience death.

Agnostic but open to the alleged truths and abilities ascribed to Jesus, I felt that if there was any validity to the dictum that He was immortal, He just might hear my petition and help resolve my intense quandary. If not, then nothing would happen and I'd grow tired and fall asleep just like any other night. But one thing was certain as I lay there imploring Him: I was ready to risk my life to encounter death as it really was. Whether it would be oblivion and total extinction, or some manner of life about which I hadn't the remotest idea, I was ready.

Lying ever so still, I waited. Moments passed and all was silent; then to my surprise, I began to feel a strange warmth permeate my body. This feeling produced a profound sense of comfort and peace.

After a few moments suspended in this state, I felt a lightening of my body's weight, which continued until I felt almost weightless. Then suddenly, I felt an instantaneous surge of great electrical energy stemming from my feet, moving up my entire body and culminating with a sense of pressure and fullness in my head. "This is it!" I thought. "He's taken me at my word."

The fullness in my head increased to where I thought it would explode, and then, with the sensation of a powerful magnet, I felt my eyes drawn inward with such a force that my eyes felt as if they'd become inverted. At that precise point, I was out of my body, separated and hovering a foot or two above my physical form. "So this is death," I thought with exhilaration. I laughed in the fabulous discovery that there was no death after all, and therefore, no need for fearing it.

Once I accepted the fact that I'd undergone the actual death experience, I hovered in space, feeling grateful for the continuity of my consciousness. I was a thinking, feeling, living, conscious entity, independent of the physical body. What a marvelous discovery!

Then a new thought emerged: "Will this lucid consciousness be a permanent part of me, or might it slowly diminish into nothingness in time?" With that thought, a twinge of doubt and fear entered me.

Instantly, I felt a presence along my right side, and heard a female voice: "Remain calm." I recognized this voice, and having trust in her guidance, I obediently relaxed as she'd advised. I could feel my doubt and fear diminishing. She then said, "Surrender yourself completely."

With trust, I honored her request and relaxed. As soon as I did this, all fear vanished and I began to slowly move, floating upward toward the right corner of the ceiling. While ascending, I took note of the fact that all my material surroundings were in proper perspective, just as if I were physically levitating, and that my movement or immobility seemed directly related to my thoughts and emotional state. Fear and doubt produced immobility, while faith and trust propelled me.

As I neared the right corner of my ceiling, I hesitated again, taking in the strange sensation of being blocked on all sides. I decided to look around the room, then down and backward to the bed in which I had lain only a few moments earlier. Lying motionless there was a body, a body that was supposed to be me, but wasn't. I felt detached from it, and couldn't have cared less. I discarded it as easily as a hand would discard a glove after entering a warm room because it was no longer needed.

I knew at that moment that my real essence, the true me, existed without a body. Feeling satisfied and secure in this knowledge, I decided to continue ascending. I floated up through and beyond the ceiling, above the house and trees and into the night sky. The freedom I felt was overwhelming, as was my awe at the wonder of it all.

I continued rising higher and higher, like a helium balloon, into space. After ascending so high that all things material were no longer visible to me, I wondered where I was going. It was as if I were entering a void, empty of all objects, designs, images, sights, sounds, and colors. There was only my lucid consciousness of being, that and magnanimous feelings of peace, love, joy, and bliss. It was unfathomable, as unimaginable ecstasy filled me. I could have remained there forever.

And it seems I did remain in this blissful, contemplative state for quite some time, content, assuming I'd arrived at my destination—the core and summit of the death experience. I was surprised at what happened next.

My spiritual body, in which I'd been traveling since exiting my physical form, began to disintegrate as I felt my being melt, spreading out into the vastness of the All. The All, without beginning or end, extended limitlessly, filling all space. I realized I was a part of this space, just as it was a part of me. I was bodiless, timeless, weightless, pure mind and spirit, merging so perfectly with spirit that I was left with the feeling of complete oneness. Never before or since have I ever felt a state of such immeasurable emotional happiness. Surely this was the Heaven that all humans dream about, that few really believed in, and that most (including myself) never thought possible to experience.

How long I remained in this euphoric state, I do not know. But after a time, I felt a gentle but distinct magnetic force nudging, then pulling me, away and downward at an angle. As I separated from the void, I withdrew into myself and once again became an individualized spiritual form. I realized I was moving toward another level or location.

I was being drawn to the opening of what appeared to be a very black tunnel. I abruptly stopped outside the tunnel's entrance, deliberating whether I had the courage to let myself pass through this blackness or not. Where would it lead to? How long would it take? What was at the other end? Questions besieged my inquisitive mind. I didn't know, and twinges of that old fear of the unknown began creeping up inside me.

As I hesitated, I sensed this tunnel was a specific exit from our solar system or universe. I knew it would lead me to another location or level of consciousness, to another type of place or world where there would be much light and an existence far more beautiful than and superior to that of Earth. Yet, I didn't know for certain, because knowing can only result from experience, and I hadn't experienced it yet.

Considering the wondrous results experienced thus far, I felt myself leaning strongly toward taking the risk when I was startled by the voice I had heard earlier. "If you go through here, you cannot return!" I was stunned. Not once had I considered that a return to my body and the Earth was possible. I had been astounded to learn I could leave my body and continue to think, feel, and exist; so can you imagine the impact upon learning I could reenter at will and resume my earthly life if I chose? This was miraculous. Once I heard these words spoken by this all-loving, protective figure, there was no doubt. Her words were a revelation of the highest order, yet they made my final decision harder to make.

I felt her warm presence beside me as she patiently awaited my answer. What a conflict! The more I deliberated, the harder it was to arrive at a permanent resolution. I knew I preferred the out-of-body existence to the one of being imprisoned within the physical body. At the same time, the prospect of exploring the unknown through the black tunnel left me uncertain.

Suddenly, I was thrust forward in time and found myself suspended in midair over my bed in my bedroom. The room was flooded with morning light, and I knew it was the next day. My body was still lying in the same position on the bed, still and seemingly lifeless.

I heard a sound at the base of the stairwell and knew it was my parents. I saw them as they ascended the stairs. As they approached the top, my mother's face wrenched in horror as she looked upon my lifeless body, and I heard her scream.

Instantaneously, I was back at the entrance to the tunnel. My decision had been made. I would go back. I would return. I would prevent the horrible anguish I was shown was certain to occur with my parents if I didn't. I realized the flash-forward experience had been given to me to aid my decision. I had never considered what pain my parents would endure from my death. To gain my happiness and freedom at the expense of another's would be wrong and selfish, I decided.

So, in response to the "voice," my quandary resolved, I said, "No, not yet." With the speed of lightning, I was back in my physical body.

I was awed and bewildered with what I had just experienced. I felt I'd been given a priceless gift to be cherished and revered all the days of my life. A revelation and experience that I knew could revolutionize my life, thoughts, ideals, values, and beliefs.

At the moment of reentry, something deep within me uttered, "This is the way an immaculate conception takes place." What a magnificent thought. I wondered if it could be true. If it was, perhaps there was a great deal more truth about the life of Jesus than I'd ever thought possible.

As I lay there trying to comprehend the wonder of it all, I didn't know whether to be glad or sad over my return. Part of me felt sadness and regret in leaving the spiritual abode behind. Yet gratitude and joy sprang up in me as I realized that no matter what my earthly life entailed, I knew what to expect at my journey's end. I smiled.

I felt a chill, and attempting to move my hands and fingers, discovered I was unable to move them for a few minutes. Initially, they felt icy and rigid, but gradually, their warmth and dexterity were restored.

How I longed to rejoice and tell the world what I had experienced, but I knew I would not until the day came when I could find at least one independent, credible source and witness to validate it.

Is it true that "in patience we possess our souls"? It surely must be, for the validation I sought was finally forthcoming through the pioneering work of psychiatrist Raymond A. Moody, Jr., M.D., in his well-documented book, *Near Death and Clinical Death*. He gathered experiences from more than a thousand case histories since 1976.

Having gone through two near-death experiences later in my life (the first in 1955 following a ruptured appendix and the second in 1957 from profuse hemorrhaging), I can testify to the fact that whether from illness, injury, or mental inducement, one's state of being outside the body is amazingly consistent among individuals reporting the experience.

The important aspect to consider is that we have a second body within us—the "body" of the soul, composed of spirit, mind, will, and emotions, and through which we can function independently of our physical body, here, now and forever!

Faye Wolff-Allen

Excerpt from the author's autobiography, The Third Testament —A New Revelation, *Vantage Press, NY*

Bonnie

My friend Bonnie and I were very close for seventeen years. We both had weight problems, and on Tuesday nights we would go to TOPS, a Weight Watchers-type place, and weigh in. Bonnie began to drop weight fast—too fast. She began to have stomach pain and finally went to a doctor.

The news was not good. Bonnie had colon cancer. She only lived another nine months. I would see or call her every day. They were going to put her in hospice, and she called for me to come visit her. We had a lovely time, and she did not appear to be in pain. When I was leaving, she asked me to hold her hands and pray with her. Instead, I said, "Bonnie, when you get to Heaven, look for my daughter, Debbie, and let me know how each of you are!" I left her, and one week later she passed on.

About ten days after her death, I went into a store to get a sympathy card. As I started to pick one up, a funny feeling came over me. I knew from past experiences that I should follow my feelings. I went to the book section for a detective story and saw *The Messengers*. I took the book home, and as I was reading it, I decided the time to act was now. Before I went to bed, I prayed that Bonnie would get in touch with me. I put my trust in the angelic presence to show up at exactly 4:44.

I woke up each night after I read the book, but I did not look at the clock. One night, I did look. I woke up and lay in bed thinking I must have lost my marbles. But I got up and took the cover off the clock. It was 4:47. I laughed and said, "You angels are a little late." I went back to sleep and in the morning, it dawned on me that the angels were not late; I was late. I had lain in bed for three minutes before I had looked at the clock. From that point on, the 444s appeared regularly in my life.

One week later, Oren, my husband, and I were taking care of some errands, and our conversation turned to Bonnie. It was a Tuesday, and every Tuesday evening Bonnie and I had gone to weigh in, then stop for supper. I told Oren how much I missed her, as we had been so close. I felt a presence there in my home. I could not see anything or anyone, but I knew Bonnie was there. I turned around and faced the clock. It was 4:44 P.M.

Since then, there have been many times I've known Bonnie and Debbie were with me.

Sylvia Heckert

Afterword

The stories shared with you in this book have come from people from all walks of life, but they all have one thing in common. The people who wrote these stories had an experience regarding the transition of the spirit and soul of a loved one that had a major impact on their lives.

They have shared these stories so you may have comfort in knowing that there is no such thing as death, but only a transition of the spirit. We are sure that many of you have also had spiritual experiences surrounding the death of your own loved ones and that these experiences could have a major impact on others. Your story could inspire others, give them hope, and help them through their grieving period, so we would like to hear from you. The stories selected would appear in a sequel to this book.

Send us your story and any comments you may have regarding this book to:

The Great Tomorrow
P.O. Box 2222
Lake Oswego, OR 97035

God bless you as you continue on your journey.

Nick Bunick

Index

About the Artist

Dispeller of Darkness was painted for a show in Portland, Oregon. As I started to paint with soft, watery colors, darker purples and blues wanted to be present. Finally, going with the deeper tones, angels came to the surface, revealing their power, dispelling the darkness, letting the light shine through.

Dispeller of Darkness is available as a 16" x 20" print. To receive a catalog of cards and prints call 1-800-685-1895.

—*Ann Rothan*

About the Author

Once he was a successful businessman. He owned several corporations, sat on the boards of others, and had a high profile in the business world. Then, in 1995, all that changed for Nick Bunick when the angelic world intervened in his life and reminded him of his mission. Part of that mission was to found The Great Tomorrow, a non-profit corporation committed to spiritual and humanitarian activities. Bunick publishes a monthly newsletter about Great Tomorrow projects, and he travels widely and lectures on his spiritual insights. In 1998, Hampton Roads published his book, *In God's Truth*. Currently, Nick, who lives in Lake Oswego, Oregon, is working with producers to develop a movie based on his life and spiritual views as retold in the best-selling book, *The Messengers*, written by Julia Ingram and G.W. Hardin.

Hampton Roads Publishing Company

. . . for the evolving human spirit

Hampton Roads Publishing Company
publishes books on a variety of subjects including
metaphysics, health, complementary medicine,
visionary fiction, and other related topics.

For a copy of our latest catalog,
call toll-free, 800-766-8009,
or send your name and address to:

Hampton Roads Publishing Company, Inc.
1125 Stoney Ridge Road
Charlottesville, VA 22902
e-mail: hrpc@hrpub.com
www.hrpub.com